HOW TO SUCCEED IN H

JOHN McKENNA

# HOW TO
# succeed in hospitality

### John McKenna

**ESTRAGON PRESS**

FIRST PUBLISHED IN 2004

BY ESTRAGON PRESS, DURRUS, COUNTY CORK

© ESTRAGON PRESS LTD, 2004

TEXT © JOHN McKENNA

ISBN 1 874076 56 1

PRINTED IN SPAIN BY GRAPHYCEMS

All rights reserved. No part of this publication may be reproduced or utilised in any form by any means, electronic or mechanical, including photocopying, recording or by any information storage and retrieval system, without prior written permission of the publishers. The author has asserted his moral rights.

PUBLISHING EDITOR: SALLY McKENNA

DESIGN: NICK CANN

EDITOR: JUDITH CASEY

COVER PHOTOGRAPHY: MIKE O'TOOLE

WEB: FLUIDEDGE

# www.bridgestoneguides.com

FOR DARINA ALLEN

WHO HAS EDUCATED SO MANY IN THE ART OF HOSPITALITY

**with thanks to:**

adriaan bartels, paul carroll, shelagh conway, orlaith cussen, donagh davern, evan doyle, catherine fulvio, bill kelly, dan mullane, patrick o'flaherty, deirdre o'neill, padraig treacy

and
frank mckevitt, mike o'toole, nick cann, judith casey, chris carroll,
josette cadoret, hugh stancliffe, miguel sancho

# Contents

| | |
|---|---|
| INTRODUCTION | 11 |
| 1. THE FUTURE OF HOSPITALITY | 17 |
| 2. CREATING A DESTINATION | 25 |

## The four addresses    49

- 3. BED, AND BREAKFAST    **49**
- 4. THE HOUSE IN THE COUNTRY    **97**
- 5. HOTELS AND HOW TO RUN THEM    **107**
- 6. RESTAURANTS WITH ROOMS    **127**

| | |
|---|---|
| 7. THE ART OF DESIGN | 135 |
| 8. THE WELL-TRAVELLED HOST | 143 |
| 9. MARKETING AND MEDIA | 153 |

| | |
|---|---|
| APPENDIX & RECIPES | 167 |
| BIBLIOGRAPHY | 182 |
| INDEX | 184 |

## INTRODUCTION

"How much depends upon the way things are presented in this world can be seen from the very fact that coffee drunk out of wine glasses is really miserable stuff."

G. C. LICHTENBERG

# INTRODUCTION

Hospitality is founded on the art of service.

With great service, the most simple place to stay can be eminent and luxurious. With great service, a guest feels pampered, respected, understood, indulged. With great service, a guest feels emotionally engaged.

With great service, an everyday experience – staying in an hotel during a conference, staying in a B&B when travelling in the country, meeting a colleague for dinner in a restaurant with rooms – can become a transcendent experience, something that lifts the traveller out of the quotidian, something that makes the traveller feel invigorated and inspired.

It is service that unifies all the elements of hospitality. Whether you are running a grand city hotel, a tiny B&B, a sprawling country house or a simple restaurant with rooms, the multifarious elements that you must master, from cooking to cleaning, via sorting out the technology to landscaping the grounds, are all unified for the guest by the act of service. Great service creates loyal customers, and loyal customers are the backbone and the bread and butter of successful hospitality enterprises.

## "Hospitality, n. The virtue which induces us to feed and lodge certain persons who are not in need of food and lodging."

**AMBROSE BIERCE**

# INTRODUCTION

Ambrose Bierce's wickedly witty quote from his famous *Devil's Dictionary*, may seem like a slightly scabrous attack on the business of hospitality. It seems to suggest that hospitality is futile. After all, why give someone something of which they have no obvious need?

But Bierce's wicked little jab does actually hit the nail on the head: when he describes hospitality as a "virtue".

For so it is: hospitality is a virtue, one of the great human virtues, and what is more, the business of hospitality is also a vocation. Treat it like a job, and you will fail, for hospitality demands more of the person engaged in it than simply jumping through the hoops and then punching in your card and going home and forgetting about it all.

Hospitality may be expressed via the art of service, but fundamentally hospitality is the expression of a personality. If you meet those people who are the masters of the art of hospitality, you also meet people who are utterly, compellingly, fascinating individuals. Hospitality may be their job, but it is also their *métier*, their art form.

Much as the best restaurateurs transcend the essentially simple business of cooking food for others, the masters of hospitality transcend the difficult business of providing hospitality for their guests.

And in so doing, they create something that is irresistible, no matter how simple, no matter how lavish, no matter how complex it may be. This is why we want hospitality: having no need of it, we recognise that it is one of the most significant luxuries. That is why it is virtuous of people to offer it to us: they could choose to do something else other than looking after

## INTRODUCTION

us, and choosing to do things that, fundamentally, we could do for ourselves. Hospitality, then, is the ultimate luxury brand.

This book attempts to examine the vital details of running a successful hospitality business, but it doesn't actually tell you where to put the broadband connectors, or why you should always use white towels, though it will tell you how to scramble eggs and make muesli and what sort of music you might consider choosing to play at breakfast-time.

I have grappled with the question of broadband plugs and white towels in various consultancy projects, but that has simply taught me that every single project in hospitality demands individual answers that are specific to each building and each concept.

There are no general answers to the multifarious questions that lie ahead of every hospitality project, and you will have to sort out the nuts and bolts each and every time you do something new.

But, if there are no general answers to the individual intricacies of each hospitality project, there are general themes that underlie the business of hospitality, and it is those general themes that this book sets out to explore.

Service unifies all the elements of hospitality, but everyone in the business needs to have an appreciation of exactly what these key elements are. If you never advert to the fact that private guests in your hotel have different demands to conference or wedding guests, those private clients will never return to your hotel.

If you fail to understand that providing a country house experience is about more than simply offering someone a nice

# INTRODUCTION

room in a nice house and cooking them a nice dinner, then you will never achieve your potential, never mind exceed it.

If your bed and breakfast offers a dull, uninspiring breakfast, don't be surprised if you never see those guests again. And, if your restaurant with rooms has superb rooms but less than superb cooking, you are headed down a one-way street to liquidation.

Hospitality succeeds when it offers the guest what they want, and then some. Knowing what they want, and then knowing how to provide it, is the art of hospitality. Like any other art form, it demands intuition, experience, and commitment. Inspiration without the perspiration won't cut it.

And, as many of the testimonies from people in the hospitality industry quoted in this book point out, hospitality is a 24/7 job. If you aren't prepared for that, don't even consider hospitality as a career.

"I adore pleasing people" is how the enormously successful Australian chef Bill Granger describes his motivation, in the introduction to his book *Bill's Open Kitchen*. That is a succinct and elegant summary of just what you need to succeed in hospitality. Pleasing people is the *modus operandi* of the business, and in hospitality you please people through the art of service, thereby creating the ultimate luxury brand.

JOHN McKENNA
DURRUS, COUNTY CORK, JANUARY 2004

# 1

# THE FUTURE OF HOSPITALITY

# 1

"Yesterday's avant garde experience
is today's chic and tomorrow's cliché."

RICHARD HOFSTADER

# THE FUTURE OF HOSPITALITY

In hospitality, nothing stands still, nothing stays the same.

As the American historian Richard Hofstader has written: "Yesterday's avant garde experience is today's chic and tomorrow's cliché".

Ouch! Does it all really happen that fast? The answer is: yes. What people want, and the way in which they want it, or think they want it, is in a state of permanent flux. Trying to satisfy this ever changing, ever-evolving need is extraordinarily demanding for people in the business of hospitality. Being hip with design or architecture or gizmos or gewgaws is no longer enough: someone will be along in a week or a month who will be hipper than you were last week or last month.

I mean, what is the point in creating the 10 million euro spa if someone is just about to unveil their 15 million euro spa? Plasma screen TVs? They're everywhere. ISDN lines? Already a cliché. State-of-the-art conference centre? Yeah, yeah. Dog pampering services? Techno-butlers? A pillow menu? Where will it all end?

Actually, it will all end where it all began: with genuine, true, efficient and courteous hospitality. The problem, as I see it, is that if you set off on the business of having the biggest, hippest, hottest, most up-to-the-minute whatever, if you get wrapped up in that competitive game, if you meander off the track of being focused on service for your guests, then you are actually set on a road to nowhere.

If you are determined to be avant garde today, then tomorrow will see you being no more than chic, and you are staring cliché in the face. That is the hospitality equivalent of the rat race.

But, let's say that you decide not to do all that jazz. Let's say

## THE FUTURE OF HOSPITALITY
### avant garde • chic • cliché

that with your B&B, your country house, your hotel or your restaurant with rooms – heck, even with your neat little motel – that you don't want to wind up a cliché, then what should you do? You want longevity, satisfaction, pleasure and a decent profit from your business. Does the future of hospitality offer you any future?

The answer is: yes! As the fashion writer Vanessa Friedman has recently pointed out, "In a world where the luxury hotel was fast becoming as common as the chain brand, the way forward was *savoir-faire*."

*Savoir-faire?* "Quickness to know and do the right thing; tact." Yes, that will do nicely.

Quickness in knowing how to do the right thing, and tact in doing it, is the sort of motto that will take any hospitality business forward.

Ms Friedman was writing about an experience in Paris's famous Hotel de Crillon, where she set the staff a test: could they produce a list of the best shops in Paris from which she could source children's clothes? The hotel came up trumps: a list of sixteen clothes shops and five shoe shops was waiting when Ms Friedman arrived. But, more importantly, the staff had also marked their personal favourites. "Such local advice, unsolicited, is priceless."

Star quality in hospitality, therefore, lies in "the more abstract extras of information and access". Information and access, that is what you need to offer.

You have a hip city hotel? What your guests really want to gain access to is the smart clubs and parties. You need to have the info, and the ability to get them access. A party of fishermen

## THE FUTURE OF HOSPITALITY
avant garde • chic • cliché

desperate to hook a fish? Same story: you need to know exactly where they need to wade in order to get the result. A food lover who is desperate to sample the best local restaurants, especially that place written up in last month's *Linoleum*\*™ magazine? You need to have the sort of relationship with your hot local restaurateur that gets your guest a table at the last minute. You need the information that gets the access.

Knowing local history and historical sites? It has to be in your portfolio. The best gardens to visit, beaches to swim at, walks to embark upon, pubs to visit, craft shops and galleries that must be checked out, markets to visit, artisan food specialities that guests should think of bringing home with them? All of this has to be in your ken.

What you have to become, to take a term from a short story by the Argentinian writer Jorge Luis Borges, is an aleph: you are the point from which, for the guest, all aspects of the universe can be seen. For the guest who, more than anything else, wants to be looked after, you are the vital means of information and access that will make their time with you special. Looking after them means taking them inside your bailiwick.

The finest practitioners of hospitality do this instinctively,

> "WE ARE TIRED OF
> SUFFERING FOR THEIR ART."
>
> NOTA BENE

## THE FUTURE OF HOSPITALITY
### avant garde • chic • cliché

seemingly as if they have an extra sense, the ability to know what the customer wants, what the customer needs, even before the customer themselves knows precisely what they want or what they need. Intuition, and a pretty amazing memory, will take you very far, but you can also use technology to give you a head start: every preference or demand – or complaint – expressed by a guest should be noted and logged, and when they call or mail again to make a booking, you should be able to scroll up that info on the computer.

Now, you are one step ahead. What did they like, or not like? If they are back a year after their last visit, does that mean business – the annual trade shows – or does it mean an anniversary or a birthday, a quality time visit? Or are they back exploring the flora, or the beaches, or the vineyards and restaurants?

Having this extra information lets you customise their experience, and that is the key to succeeding in the future of hospitality. And the ability to customise means that you can play to your strengths, it means that the focus of their visit is centred on your expertise, your ability to offer access and information, the inside dope that makes them feel valued, and that allows you to shine.

In the future of hospitality, the ultimate USP – the Unique Selling Point – is actually the ultimate USP – the Uniquely Special Person. The future of hospitality demands that you become that USP: the person with the *savoir-faire*. The person with the "Quickness to know and do the right thing; tact". The person with the local advice, the person who can provide the vital information, the person who can gain the vital access.

# TESTIMONY

Dan Mullane, The Mustard Seed, Adare

## To run a hotel successfully you should know how:

### 1. TO COOK...

should the chef throw in his apron.

### 2. TO WASH UP...

should the dishwasher break down.

### 3. TO WAIT ON TABLES...

should the manager break his leg.

### 4. TO BE A PSYCHOLOGIST...

when that couple who have just checked in are not talking to each other and look sad.

### 5. TO BE AN ENTERTAINER...

when the cake arrives out, to sing happy birthday to get the party going.

### 6. TO BE A JUGGLER...

with the staff rota when you are overbooked or it's a quiet night or when it's hectic and it's meant to be your night off and you have to cancel that massage and work.

### 7. TO BE PATIENT...

when the health inspector is only fulfilling their duty with the latest EU directive which is totally impractical and unworkable!

### 8. TO BE GENEROUS...

to customers, staff and designated charities and still not go bankrupt.

### 9. TO BE SENSIBLE...

enough to realise that only 5% of last night's takings are yours so don't rush out to buy a Jaguar.

### 10. WHEN TO TAKE A BREAK...

or the customers will take a break from you and never come back!!

**THE FUTURE OF HOSPITALITY**
avant garde • chic • cliché

# primer

- Savoir-faire, the quickness to know and do the right thing, and to be able to do it with appropriate tact, is a vital ingredient of succeeding in hospitality.

- Guests want to be looked after, but they especially want the inside information and the access to local knowledge that makes them feel like insiders, not just tourists.

- Information and access may sound like abstract qualities, but they are the key to creating satisfied, and ultimately loyal, customers. They are pivotal elements of successful service.

- Hospitality practitioners are alephs: the point from which the guest can see all the relevant parts of whatever it is they want to discover.

- Use technology to build a profile of your guests that will help you be well-briefed on who they are, and what they want.

# 2

**CREATING A DESTINATION**

"The finest landscape in the world is improved by a good inn in the foreground."

SAMUEL JOHNSON

# CREATING A DESTINATION

"Shortly after we had returned home from a brief trip to an hotel to do some research for this book, my five-year-old son, P.J., walked into the kitchen with a pink marker and a blank sheet of paper.

"Dad, how do you spell 'Hotels are nice?'" he asked.

And so, with me dictating and he scribbling – "Big letter or little letter?" – he wrote: "HOTELS ARE NICE." Big letters.

Five-year-old children, in my experience, have a sure feel for good hospitality. They know when and where they are treated well, and they sure know the places where they have a good time. Treat them indifferently – adults in hotels, B&B's, country houses and restaurants with rooms usually do this by not addressing children directly, and by asking their parents questions that relate to the children – and you will vanish from the child's memory and perception, never to return.

Treat them well, and the child's wistful enunciation as you are driving down the driveway towards the exit is always the same: "When can we come back?"

Creating a successful hospitality destination means doing whatever you need to do in order to get people to say to themselves: "When can we come back." If they say that, then you have succeeded in winning a customer, and you have succeeded in creating a destination address.

Being a destination for people, whether they seek leisure and pleasure or business, is how you build a business that will prosper over the long term. If your address coincides with the customer's mental map of the zone – Connemara equals place X; Killarney equals place Y; Belfast equals place Z – then your business is safe and sound and secure.

# CREATING A DESTINATION
hospitality • identity • added value

So, how on earth do you become a Destination?

This is a question we have grappled with for many years. We first began to explore different places to stay in Ireland as long ago as 1989 when writing *The Irish Food Guide*, and in 1992 we wrote and published the first edition of *The Bridgestone 100 Best Places to Stay in Ireland*.

It is worth printing the introduction to that book as a summary of what we were looking for more than a decade ago, and what we had been finding:

"The Irish are a uniquely hospitable people. Their hospitality is not only legendary, it is genuine, unforced, delightful. They have the ability to calm even the most exhausted and jaundiced traveller into a state of warm contentment in a matter of minutes, and to be able to do it instincitvely.

The cup of tea with some home-made biscuits which makes its way up to your bedroom within minutes of arriving, perhaps the belt of something stronger to revive your spirits and bring you back to life. Some fresh flowers in the room, maybe the thoughtful demand that any special requests must be made known to the proprietors straight away so that they can be accommodated. The small, but vital, details which make the difference between your stay being a time of rapture or a time of discomfort are things which the Irish can achieve without, it seems, even thinking about them.

It is a matter of social ease – the Irish are by and large unconcerned with questions of social class and status and are likely to treat one and all exactly the same – and it is also a

# CREATING A DESTINATION
## hospitality • identity • added value

matter of things as elusive as a tone of voice, an instinctive affability, easy-going social grace, the happy atmosphere of people who are happy in their work.

It is in the creation and the nurturing of this atmosphere, that relaxing, balmy, confident feeling which we all instinctively know says that something is just right and that one is destined for a good time, that the Irish excel. And it is this, above all else, that makes staying in Ireland so enjoyable, so memorable. You are made to feel special, pampered, you are allowed to relax.

When one encounters this happy set of circumstances in an Irish establishment – and we have sought out that dreamy mix of generosity, hospitality, thoughtfulness and professionalism wherever we went – then one realises that no one else, anywhere, can do it half so well as the Irish. It is the perfect backdrop for a family holiday, the perfect embrace for a romantic weekend, the perfect circumstances for corporate entertaining, or personal time out. It conjures an idyllic picture, which makes it all the more galling when one realises that, all too often, the reality has nothing to do with this image.

Ireland is full of establishments where, when you wake up in the morning, you become aware of two odours. The first is the smell of disinfectant. The second is the odour which the disinfectant is trying to hide, the smell of exhausted, rank, cooking oil being subjected to another encounter with tasteless sausages, mortified eggs and stringy bacon.

That is your "Traditional Irish" breakfast being prepared.

The breakfast is further likely to feature some coffee which, despite being in a smart pot, will be instant coffee. You will yearn for fresh soda bread. You will be given factory made, pre-

# CREATING A DESTINATION
## hospitality • identity • added value

sliced gunk. The orange juice will be orange in colour, but otherwise bear little or no relationship to the citrus fruit.

If things are truly bad, you may encounter this horror with the accompaniment of roaringly loud pop music bleating from a radio or, worse, in the company of synthetic, morning TV.

When this happens, it is more than likely that you also passed the night between some excruciatingly uncomfortable nylon sheets, in a room that featured the sort of wallpaper and furnishings that you have seen in shops but never believed anyone would actually buy. Chances are the hot water you ran for your bath ran out after two bucketfuls, and that the telephone calls you made will eventually cost you two or three pounds each. And then they will add ten percent on top of them, just to round numbers out.

This nightmare vision, this screwball adventure with your host as villain and you as the joke, happens a lot in Ireland. This book, unlike its companion volumes on Food and Restaurants, is written not just out of enthusiasm and love, but also out of a sense of dread and horror. We hope that you never stay in some of the places we have stayed in, because the thought of your misery is too upsetting.

We have looked for places to stay where the proprietors care about more than the colour of your money, places where the hospitality is true, the cleanliness is undoubted, the welcome is honest. We are, by and large, unimpressed by sheer slickness, or thoughtless luxury and that cool, distant tone which dominates up-market hotels and which owes nothing to the true character of the Irish. Instead we have sought out places that are homey, comfortable, perhaps somewhat funky. We like places where you

# CREATING A DESTINATION
## hospitality • identity • added value

can relax and not worry about the fact that you are, of course, in someone else's home.

Whilst the location of the establishments we have chosen does have something of a bearing in deciding their suitability, ultimately we have tried to find houses and farmhouses, B&Bs and hotels where the place itself is the real attraction. Ideally, one wants to find places to stay where you do no more than eat, sleep and relax in and about the place, walk in the grounds or the nearby seashore, read, eat, drink and feel blissfully merry without even thinking about getting in the car to head off here or there. A splendid place in the middle of nowhere is still a splendid place.

The owner of a country house in Galway once told us that he was often asked, by prospective guests, what amenities his house enjoyed. 'I'm pushed to think of any, really,' he replied. 'Just beautiful surroundings, good food and peace'. That seems to us to be the perfect prescription.

## WHAT DO YOU WANT TO DO?

We can summarise that introduction in a simple form: don't rely on the legend of Irish hospitality to create your Destination address: you have to work at it.

The first step, then, in creating a destination is to decide: what can I do? And what do I want to do?

The 1992 *Bridgestone Guide*, for instance, featured a restaurant with rooms that had just opened at the end of 1991. Castlemurray House, at St. John's Point near to Bruckless in

# CREATING A DESTINATION
## hospitality • identity • added value

County Donegal, owned and run by Thierry and Claire Delcros, was just setting out on a hugely successful spell, its mix of inexpensive rooms and excellent cooking earning it a reputation that is maintained to this day by its new owner, Marguerite Howley, a protégée of M. Delcros who bought Castlemurray a few years back.

Castlemurray was then something new for Ireland. Thierry Delcros was a chef, his wife ran front of house: they were restaurateurs, not hoteliers. Running a restaurant was what they knew.

But the far-flung location of Castlemurray meant that a stand-alone restaurant simply could not succeed, especially with the short tourist season in Donegal. So, M. Delcros introduced a concept he was familiar with in France: the Restaurant with Rooms.

This meant simple rooms, initially only four in number that cost relatively little, with no one to carry your bag and no room service. M. Delcros could also build the rooms himself; that was what he could also do. By the following year, the number of rooms had already increased to nine. Castlemurray was away on a hack.

One of my most vivid memories of researching for the *Bridgestone Guides* was of calling to Castlemurray years later, in the middle of winter, in the middle of a storm, when it was almost impossible to actually find the road to the restaurant the weather was so atrocious. I walked through the doors, to find that the place was packed with guests, all staying overnight, all eating in the restaurant, all having a wonderful time, thank you very much. Castlemurray had become a Destination, despite a

# CREATING A DESTINATION
hospitality • identity • added value


remote location, and despite being a concept that the Irish were, initially, unfamiliar with.

But Castlemurray played to the strengths of the owners: it allowed them to establish a successful restaurant, with the benefit of inexpensive rooms proving a huge attraction for people who wanted to chill out, have a good dinner, spend some quality time with each other, and not spend too much money. Conrad Hilton's famous dictum that the success of an hotel was dependent on "Location, location, location" had been turned upside down. Castlemurray succeeded because it let the owners do what they were good at, it allowed them to shine, whilst giving people access to the experience via the medium of affordable rooms. Its core business was repeat business, familiar customers returning to a familiar place, people for whom south Donegal is represented on their mental map by Castlemurray House, as it continues to be to this day.


## THINK LIKE WATER

You cannot create a destination, therefore, unless the set-up in which you intend to operate plays to your strengths.

If you are a cook, then create a restaurant with rooms, where your cooking remains the focus of the experience: that was the Castlemurray USP. The red-hot cooking of Neven Maguire in Cavan's MacNean Bistro explains why Mr Maguire's simple rooms are packed every weekend with travellers: these people have travelled here, to the middle of nowhere, to eat.

Not too far away in the charming Olde Post Inn, another

# CREATING A DESTINATION
## hospitality • identity • added value

restaurant with simple rooms is already established as a destination thanks to Gearoid Lynch's cooking.

If you are an especially talented designer, emphasise the design elements of the house as its USP. Many people who run well-known addresses use this as their USP. Paddy and Julia Foyle, of Connemara's celebrated Quay House, use their idiosyncratic and utterly winning way with design as their USP, and there are many more in Ireland who do the same, from Kinsale's Blindgate House to Coast Townhouse in Tramore to Ken and Cathleen Buggy's Glencairn Inn near Lismore. Top-end hotels such as The Clarence and The Morrison then take this one stage further, stressing the contribution of their designers, famous names such as Keith Hobbs and John Rocha.

If you are a particularly capable person who is excellent at conceptualising an entire experience, then the demands of a large hotel will satisfy your abilities to manage both guests and staff. Hoteliers such as Evan Doyle of The Brook Lodge Inn or Dan Mullane of Echo Lodge are superlative at the demanding demands of such an enterprise.

If you enjoy having guests, but don't have managerial experience, then focus your ambitions on running a great B&B. Violet Connell's Fortview House, near to Goleen in West Cork, may be a simple farmhouse B&B, but there is no more beloved or respected address in the country: Mrs Connell is a superlative B&B keeper, simple as that, and Fortview plays to her strengths.

If you exceed your level of competence, then nothing will so cruelly expose your limitations as the hospitality industry. You need to think very hard indeed about what you can do and, above all, what you cannot do. Think like water: find the right

# CREATING A DESTINATION
hospitality • identity • added value

level in which you are comfortable. Work out your specialisation, your USP, and stick to it.

Where I have found that addresses under-perform and ultimately fail is where someone is trying to do something that they are not particularly suited for. The country house owner who is actually shy and retiring and not a great success with dealing with guests: disaster. The restaurant with rooms where the cooking is not sharp enough so that guests overlook the simplicity of the rooms: disaster. The country house owners who

> "CONFUSING AS IT SEEMS TO US AT FIRST SIGHT, THE WORDS 'HOST' AND 'GUEST' ORIGINALLY MEANT THE SAME THING. THEY BOTH DERIVE FROM INDO-EUROPEAN GHOSTIS, 'STRANGER'. WHAT THIS SINGLE TERM REFERS TO IS NOT SO MUCH THE INDIVIDUAL PEOPLE, THE HOST AND THE GUEST, AS THE BOND THAT UNITES THEM."
>
> **MARGARET VISSER**

## CREATING A DESTINATION
### hospitality • identity • added value

have bought a big place with all the money they have made in the city, and who don't really think it should be their job to serve people dinner and open the wine: disaster. The hotelier who is unable to put together a package that is attractive to several different types of customer: disaster.

The reason why you must find your level of competence is in order that you can be successful, and in this regard, don't imagine that running a 5-star hotel is a greater achievement than running a sparkling little B&B down the country: it isn't.

Just as the smartest chefs have abolished the traditional concept of hierarchy in cooking and restaurants, so the best people in hospitality know that doing something simple to the very best of your ability is what truly makes for success.

A truffled lobster, cooked by rote, is not better than a ham sandwich made with care and love. Similarly, an hotel room kitted out at a cost of 50,000 euros by a designer and packed with all the latest gizmos and whatnots is not more comfortable than a simple but well-conceived room in a country B&B that shows the design skill of the owner.

It may be more lavish, it may be a thousand times more expensive, but only a fool will presume that it must therefore be more comfortable, more welcoming, and more enjoyable to stay in. Money cannot compensate for a lack of imagination, no matter how much money you have.

Remember, hospitality is all about imagination and instinct, about anticipation, about wanting to give pleasure, about service. If you believe that simply spending money on an address will guarantee your success, you are mistaken, and you are headed for an expensive failure.

**CREATING A DESTINATION**
hospitality • identity • added value

## DESTINATION & IDENTITY

One of the key elements of creating a destination is to create an identity for the destination. Having a beautiful house or a smart hotel is all very well, but you need to take it a step further, and ensure all the elements of your appearance work together, and that the message they transmit to your guests is seamless.

From a very simple point of view, this can be something as basic as painting the house you have bought before opening your doors to guests: you would not believe the number of places that open up and don't even take this basic step, even if the previous owners had run the place into the ground through incompetence. If you don't signal your arrival, how on earth are people to guess that there is a new regime at work?

Think of identity as your trademark: something distinct, something different, something that you want to protect, something that signals who you are and what you do.

Bryan Leech and Martin Marley, of Carlow's Kilgraney House, might answer a request for information for a new edition of the *Bridgestone Guide* by enclosing, along with details of prices and openings and a CD-rom of pictures of their latest developments, a pot of their excellent orange and passion fruit marmalade. Simple, and smart.

The label has their trademark sun symbol, and their trademark logo, which is to be found on all their stationery, along with their web address and contact details.

The real clincher, however, is the message being sent by the marmalade itself: orange is standard and commonplace in marmalade, passion fruit is not. It tells you that this creative and

# CREATING A DESTINATION
## hospitality • identity • added value

idiosyncratic pair of country house keepers pay attention to every detail, and give everything their own idiosyncratic spin: even the breakfast marmalade.

Details such as this take your trademark all the way home. In simple gestures such as this, you are creating your brand, you are creating successful marketing, you are exceeding expectations. And all you have had to do is make some labels and make some marmalade. It's not rocket science: it's common sense. If you are good at it, you can take it even further, and retail your kitchen products, as Sammy Leslie has done with the kitchen products of Castle Leslie: you will find their range for sale in Brown Thomas.

So, your stationery, your flyers, your cutlery and crockery, your crafts and furniture, even the way in which you communicate with customers, must all signal your identity. Ballymaloe House, for instance, has always used the doleful little men sketched by Mel Calman for the original Ballymaloe Cookbook as the design element of their stationery and any cards, flyers and signs they use. It's a simple thing, but extremely effective, simply because you remember it, even if you have never heard of Mel Calman.

With destination addresses, developing a good website is vital. For many customers today, in an age when people will book entire vacations without ever speaking to the people at their destinations, it is the first port of call, the first glimpse of where they want to go, their first encounter with the people who will be their hosts. And they will make up their minds about you from the quality of your website: how it looks; how easy it is to navigate, what it says not just about you but about where you

# CREATING A DESTINATION
## hospitality • identity • added value

are and what you offer. The good news is that it is no longer necessary to spend a great deal of money on websites, but the bad news is that you simply cannot afford to get it wrong. If the site looks cheesy and amateurish, then your guests – if they do make a booking – will have that presumption about you even before they arrive.

So, you must make sure that the message you are sending out is of a piece with your premises. Website. Stationery. Letterheads. Labels. The images you choose must drive home the content and character of your offer at each point, and it is all designed to create a simple effect: when the guests turn up and take a look, you want them to say: "I knew it would be like this." Mission accomplished.

## WHAT YOU DON'T DO

Identity is not just what you are: it is also what you are not. The swish new Rival Hotel in Stockholm, for instance, could choose to focus on the fact that it has lots of elements as part of its offer of a top-class hotel, including a cinema. But the hotel also defines itself this way. Caroline Eriksson, the hotel's general manager, told the writer Tyler Brulé that "There are five 'p's' we're proud not to have at the hotel. No pissoirs, pralines on the pillow, porn, popcorn or parapluies in cocktails."

So, there you go. Their USP isn't what they give; it's also what they don't give. Luxury is what they choose to exclude, rather than all the things that are included. There is wisdom in this, but you can also do it in a more practical way, simply by excluding

# CREATING A DESTINATION
## hospitality • identity • added value

from your offer the things you are not comfortable doing, or the things you feel you achieve less well.

In other words, always focus on the elements that you can achieve to the highest standard, don't try to do all things for all men, and when it comes to your identity, be brash: don't put mints on the pillows if you feel it's a dumb thing to do; don't feel you have to have CNN in every room just because you have guests from the 'States (isn't CNN what they are trying to get away from?); and think creatively: no guest remembers if someone sticks a mint on their pillow, but no guest ever forgets if someone switches on a warm bed blanket for them or – even better – slips a hot-water bottle into their bed at turn-down time. The hot-water bottle shows real imagination; the mint is just a dumb cliché.

## READING THE LANDSCAPE

Where you are will dictate the sort of destination address you can create. You have a chalet up in the hills? Focus on walking, hiking and adventure holidays. You have an hotel in West Cork? You are in vacation territory, so don't waste time trying to attract conferences: they won't travel that far to get to you because the logistics are wrong.

You are at the end of the Dingle Peninsula? Stress that your destination is an "away from it all, far from the madding crowd" address, a place to chill out. The more remote, the better: to get to the beautiful Iskeroon, you have to drive across a beach. Well, that's why you bought that 4x4, isn't it?

## CREATING A DESTINATION
hospitality • identity • added value

Great destinations match their offer with their location. Kelly's Resort Hotel in the sunny South-East stresses golf holidays and leisure with pleasure. Hanora's Cottage in the Nire Valley stresses walking and hiking breaks. Renvyle, in remote Letterfrack in Connemara, emphasises its isolation, its separateness. For Ballynahinch Castle, it's huntin', shootin' and fishin' on the estate, much as it is in Newport House or Delphi Lodge.

For The Clarence or The Morrison, the gig is being at the heart of Dublin city and its nightlife.

For Otto and Hilda Kunze in Otto's Creative Catering in West Cork, the attraction is simply that of the natural world: pure, natural, local, organic food in a wildly beautiful and elemental place, a house where pigs and chickens roam in the grounds, where wild foods are collected for dinner, a place where you can connect with yourself.

But, not everyone is fortunate enough to have an address in a wild, wonderful part of the country. What to do, then, to create a destination? The answer is that you have to add in Added Value.

## ADDED VALUE

In an age when the world and his wife seem to be busy spending large fortunes on spas, it is salutary to remember that Declan and Bernadette Fagan, of Temple Spa in Horseleap, County Galway, made their house a destination thanks to a series of spa treatments which they developed slowly, organically and successfully.

# CREATING A DESTINATION
## hospitality • identity • added value

They began by offering treatments along with healthy menus, and have developed the business, creating more spa rooms and treatments as the business developed. Rather than simply dropping a spa from out of the sky at astronomical cost, they created a customer base and then offered those customers an ever-increasing range of services. The fact that the house is kind of in the middle of nowhere didn't matter: they had an Added Value attraction.

Ballymaloe House has unquestionably benefited from the reputation of the Ballymaloe Cookery School: many students at the shorter courses choose to stay at the House, so both elements of the business prosper. In Ghan House, Paul Carroll offers a cookery school with guest chefs, another attraction alongside the lovely mediaeval village of Carlingford where the house is situated, another complement to the house's reputation for good hospitality and good cooking.

But these addresses are usually the exception, and creating Added Value is still under-utilised in Ireland. With houses and hotels far from the major cities, it continues to amaze me that owners do not aim to extend their seasons by offering cookery classes, nature courses, painting and craft vacations.

How might they do this? By looking at what talents are held by people in the vicinity. Are there basketmakers nearby? Expert gardeners? Local historians? Field sports guides? Golf professionals? Water sports educators? Painters and illustrators and potters and jewellery makers?

All of these people can be your allies in forging Added Value, and remember that they will benefit from being part of the action. The goal in modern tourism is not just to attract people

## CREATING A DESTINATION
hospitality • identity • added value

to your address, but to attract them to your region, your area, and to keep them there for as long as you can possibly manage. The longer they stay, and the more elements of the local area that they can engage in and gain access to, then the more they spend, and the better a time they will have. And, once they have a good time, then they will be back.

### WOW! & WOM!

Destination addresses need to create a Wow! factor that will create a WOM! factor: the best places not only knock you out, they also send people away ready to tell all their friends about what they have just enjoyed: Word Of Mouth.

WOM is the greatest advertising and marketing tool you can have, but without a Wow! factor you will find it hard to achieve.

### MY DREAM OF YOU

A destination address gives people something that they dream about, something they have imagined and wished for, even if they don't quite realise that they wish for it.

In this regard, a true destination first of all meets people's expectations, and a truly successful destination then exceeds those expectations.

Holidaymakers, for instance, have a clear mental picture of the sort of place where they want to stay. They have an image of a

# CREATING A DESTINATION
## hospitality • identity • added value

B&B, or an hotel, and they are truly happy when reality coincides with their dream picture. Tourism is, essentially, a nostalgic pursuit, and our touristic images are always nostalgic.

We all have a picture in our minds of these archetypes of the touristic imagination, and smart people in hospitality tap into those archetypes, and offer elements and versions of them: the country cottage B&B bedecked with flowers at the entrance; the restaurant with rooms up in the mountains where the walkers and hikers can return after a day's exertion to a good dinner and drinks in the bar; the swish and hip city hotel with its cutting-edge design and cool staff members; the country house nestling in its enfolding acres with huntin', shootin' and fishin' on the agenda; the resort hotel by the beach with its swirl of white sand exaggerated by a blue sea and a distant horizon.

But business people, or conference delegates, also have a clear picture of how they want their destination to be. Their picture may be less nostalgic, less romantic, it may be rather hardheaded, but it is no less vivid. Like the romance of the holidaymaker, the hard-working citizen wants to stay someplace that coincides with the mental picture they have of their work and their life-style. Where the holidaymaker wants to feel that they are away from it all, the business player wants to feel that they are at the centre of everything: the hub of the city; the heart of the deal; the metropolitan experience writ large.

Creating a destination means – literally – reading these people's minds. What do they want? How do they want it? How can I provide it? How do I make sure that when the guest is leaving, whether they have been at work or at play, that their immediate thought is: "I want more of this."

**CREATING A DESTINATION**
hospitality • identity • added value

# primer

- Don't imagine for a moment that you can rely on the legendary hospitality of the Irish to wing along on low standards: you can't. Every hospitality destination is created out of hard work and high standards.

- Forget "Location, location, location". You can create a successful destination address anywhere you like, so long as you create a place that plays to your strengths.

- Deciding exactly what it is that you want to do, and working at a level of commitment and expertise that you are comfortable with, is the first step to success.

- Think like water: find the right level for you and your business to work at.

- Running a 5-star hotel isn't a greater achievement than running a pristine B&B. All success is relative to the ambitions of the owner and the crew.

## CREATING A DESTINATION
hospitality • identity • added value

- **No amount of money spent will compensate for a lack of imagination when it comes to design.**

- **A strong identity for your destination is vital, and it must be evident at every part of your offer, from stationery to signature style.**

- **Make a virtue of what you don't do: it's as much of a definition for your address as the things that you do offer.**

- **The location of your destination must be considered when creating your offer: corporate conferences don't happen in West Cork.**

- **Always consider the ways in which you can add value to your offer.**

- **The Wow! factor creates the WOM factor.**

- **Great destinations are dream destinations.**

# TESTIMONY

**Bill Kelly, Kelly's Resort Hotel, Rosslare**

- I wished life in the Hospitality Industry was as easy as following 10 points to success.
- What I feel drives the many successful hospitality businesses in this country, is that we are never finished searching for that "success".
- Below I have tried to outline the 10 fundamental points that have assisted the growth of Kelly's Resort over the last century.
- Mostly they are related to creating customer-focused structures.

## 1. LOCATION

The famous quotation of Conrad Hilton, "location, location, location" plays an important role in every business.

## 2. THE CUSTOMER

It is vital to create a customer-focused structure. Customer satisfaction is essential to encourage repeat business. You must offer "value for money" no matter what end of the market you work in.

## 3. THE STAFF

You can build a "palace" but you need people to operate it.
Only the people or staff make one hotel different from the next. This is especially important with dwindling differentiation in the hotel industry and increased global branding.

## 4. WORKING AS A TEAM /ROLE MODELLING

- A team creates better communication between management and staff.

- A team solves problems quickly.

- Create a flat structure where everyone works for a common aim.

- Management must display customer service.

- Listen to feed-back from customers.

- Hands-on involvement by all is vital.

## 5. AUTHORITY TO FRONT-LINE STAFF

- Give authority to front-line staff in order that they can make decisions within their sphere of responsibility.

# TESTIMONY

- Front-line staff are an essential link to the customer: trust them.

- Encourage flexibility of decisions.

- Encourage "moments of truth" or "wow!" moments.

## 6. RELATIONSHIP WITH THE CUSTOMER

- Develop guest recognition (names on tables).

- Encourage interaction between staff and guests (soccer, golf.)

- Create a genuine sense of care (flowers....)

- Encourage interaction and friendships between customers.

- Adopt a positive attitude to handling complaints. (View complaints as an opportunity.)

- Understand the lifetime value of a customer.

## 7. STAFF SELECTION/ STAFF TRAINING

Select staff with the right attitude, they can learn new skills!

On-going training is essential to improve or maintain standards.

## 8. STAFF RETENTION

- There is no formula for staff retention, but an overall mixture of ideas, actions, financial reward and a sense of genuine care are essential.

- Familiar staff makes customers feel at home!

- One of the best rewards of doing any type of work is job satisfaction and a genuine sense of self-worth.

## 9. INNOVATION/ REINVESTMENT

- Continuous improvement of the product is essential, if we are to maintain standards.

- Every company's growth starts to plateau at some stage. It is important to encourage further growth by renewing and innovating prior to any decline in business.

## 10. PROFIT

- It's the ultimate measure or ingredient for success. Without it we cannot prosper and grow.

# 3

## BED, AND BREAKFAST

"O breakfast! O breakfast! The meal of my heart!
Bring porridge, bring sausage, bring fish for a start
Bring kidneys and mushrooms and partridge's legs –
But let the foundation be bacon and eggs."

**A P HERBERT**

# BED, AND BREAKFAST

The B&B experience is quite unlike any other experience in hospitality, and for a simple reason.

Staying in an Irish bed and breakfast, you are staying in a private house, the family home of the person who is your host. And yet, unlike a normal guest invited to the house in the course of friendship or business, the relationship is a professional one: you are paying to stay.

The B&B, therefore, is a halfway house in terms of hospitality. It is domestic, yet semi-professional. It is an intimate, almost personal transaction, yet it is founded on a monetary basis. You are in a family home, yet you are not part of the family. You are a paying guest, but the services do not usually include dinner, normally the first demand of any traveller.

And yet, the B&B concept is truly the heartbeat of Irish hospitality. The fact of gaining access to a family home is a truly significant aspect of the encounter, for it takes one beyond the professional relationships that are explicit in hotels and restaurants with rooms, and into an altogether different sphere of hospitality: more intimate, less focused on financial gain, simpler and more spontaneous.

In this sense, the B&B experience is an uncanny echo of the traditional welcome afforded to the stranger, for which the Irish were so celebrated through the centuries. What mattered, and what continues to matter, is the hospitality shown by the host: this is the core of the relationship. The simplicity of the house, the simplicity of the food, is of lesser import than the generosity of the host in sharing their home.

No hotel room feels even remotely like a room in a B&B or a country house, even as the standards demanded of B&Bs and

# BED, AND BREAKFAST

country houses have been raised by astounding degrees in recent years; when we first started writing the *Bridgestone Guides*, en suite bathrooms were a rarity. Our illustrator once summed up the level of services available in many B&Bs with a pithy drawing of a shower unit. The control had three choices: Freeze. Drip. Scald. We know that shower well. Very well.

Today, things are very different. B&B keeping has been raised to an art form, and what an intense, intricate art form it is. At its best, B&B hosts are the very best practitioners of hospitality, almost literally giving everything of themselves to the task and, therefore, to the guest.

The stories of their over-delivering are legendary: the crazy, last-minute dash all the way to the airport to deliver the bunch of keys the departing traveller had left behind; the casual mention of a favourite food, only to discover the following morning that it is served to you at breakfast; the hot water bottle that has been snuggled between the sheets of your bed to await your return; we even know of one B&B keeper who realised, to his horror, shortly before the arrival of a wheelchair-bound guest, that the door to the guest's bathroom was not of adequate width: the guest arrived to find him, with sledge-hammer, widening the door. Whatever it takes.

The best thing about Irish B&Bs is that whilst standards of service and cooking have risen – often thanks to the sterling work of Darina Allen and her team at the Ballymaloe Cookery School with their hugely successful B&B courses – the traditional virtues of hospitality, modesty, courtesy and generosity have not diminished. For without the generosity of spirit that truly animates the relationship between host and

## BED, AND BREAKFAST
the bed

guest in a B&B, the experience can be depressingly uninspiring, simply because you do not feel genuinely welcome. But when that spirit is alive and kicking, then staying in an Irish B&B is one of the great experiences of hospitality and travelling that you can enjoy. Let's look at the bits and pieces of the experience: the bed, and the breakfast.

## THE BED

Making a bed demands skill, because your ambition should be to create something that is the epitome of comfort. We once made a television programme, in which we devoted part of the footage to showing Cathleen Buggy, of Buggy's Glencairn Inn, making up one of the beds that is such a trademark of the Inn.

Plump with pillows, replete with freshly-laundered sheets, swaddled with throws and covers, the old iron bed Mrs Buggy made up was transformed into the most desirable object you have ever seen.

Intensely tactile and sensual and, above all, welcoming and promisingly luxurious, the bed showed exactly the same sort of care and attention to detail that the Buggys also lavish on breakfast: it was an experience, not just a place to lay your head, just as breakfast in Buggy's is a feast, not merely a start to the day.

Many people, however, get too caught up in the orthopedic mattress spec, or the allergy-free pillow worry, or whether they should have French antique sleigh beds or modern free-standing minimalist beds, and lose sight of the fact that making the bed

## BED, AND BREAKFAST
### the bed

up to be an object in itself – the focus and centrepiece of the room – is what you should really be aiming to achieve.

Your beds should aim to be a USP of your address: different from any others, just as your breakfast should be individual and distinctive. And whilst hotels and others have concentrated on groovy designs of beds, and lavishly designed headboards, I think the secret for a B&B actually lies in how the bed is made up, for that is where you can best achieve tactility.

You want to achieve the sort of dreamy result described by the writer Reggie Nadelson: "All those pillows. All that drapery. All those people who make it up every morning with fresh linens…"

High-quality sheets are essential (many people in hospitality source their sheets from the splendid Murray's department store, in Charleville, in North County Cork, a legendary address for simple, old fashioned fabrics); tactile pillows and lots and lots of them; throws that can be either slinky or earthy; and provide a colour contrast between the white sheets and a colourful throw.

If you do all this, and surround the bed with subtle but effective lighting and appropriate bedside tables, then you have created something that achieves a status somewhere between a shrine and a grotto: a special place.

> "ONCE UPON A TIME A BED WAS A BED, MORE OR LESS. NOW A BED IS YOUR COCOON, YOUR NEST, YOUR RETREAT."
>
> **REGGIE NADELSON**

**BED, AND BREAKFAST**
The Full Irish


## THE BREAKFAST: THE FULL IRISH

A friend of mine refers to the portmanteau of ingredients that comprises the traditional Irish breakfast, and their negative impact on our waistlines, as, "The Full Catastrophe".

A catastrophe the Full Irish very often is. Factory sausages, watery bacon and battery eggs, undistinguished blood puddings and shop-bought bread, a glacial tomato not cooked properly and some flaccid mushrooms, will all create a breakfast that is a travesty of the original concept.

So, what has gone wrong with the Full Irish, and how do you make it right? The answer is that you need to consider the meal in its true, traditional concept: the Full Irish is a tribute to the skills of the pork butcher. A peppery, well-made pork sausage; properly cured bacon, whether green or smoked; and fine blood puddings, are the underpinning of the meal, and if you simply grab these ingredients from a supermarket chill cabinet, you haven't a hope of making something that has signature style and flavours.

Many of the best people in the hospitality business have grasped this truth, and have begun to put it into practice. They get Gubbeen Smokehouse bacon, or some of John David Power's marvellous smoked bacon from Dungarvan, or the excellent pork products of Caherbeg Farm in Roscarbery, West Cork. If you have a good local butcher making a traditional black pudding, then get that, especially if it has the style of the best Kerry puddings from Sneem or Annascaul.

You can order Pat O'Doherty's legendary black bacon via the internet, and there is good distribution of the excellent and

## BED, AND BREAKFAST
### The Full Irish

reliable Meadowsweet organic standard eggs from Tipperary. In Northern Ireland, the sausage-making capital of the Western World, you can get truly peerless sausages and bacon from superb craft butchers, whilst Jilly Dougan's Moyallon products are of icon status.

The point is that you must source artisan quality pork products as the basis for making a successful Irish breakfast, even if they are simply the range from your best local butcher. But, whatever you do, avoid the branded pork products from the chill cabinet of the supermarket. Once you have hand-made local pork products to work with, the battle of breakfast is more than half won.

Time, then, to concentrate on the rest of the details: make sure that the tomatoes you use are of the best quality and that you cook them thoroughly: a still-hard, warm tomato is inedible, though I despair at the number of hotels who seem to think that it is good enough for breakfast. Good breakfast mushroom caps should also be properly cooked: use a little water added to the pan after you have sautéed sliced mushrooms, and cook them properly before scattering over chopped parsley. Large field mushrooms should, ideally, be baked in the oven, with a knob of butter in the centre to melt through the cap as it bakes.

The next secret ingredient is timing. Every part of the Irish breakfast cooks at a different rate and requires a different time: this is why the meal is so difficult to get right, especially when it is 8.30am and all your guests have come downstairs at exactly the same moment.

The difficulty with the Irish breakfast is also that the ingredients do not hold well: you need to be finishing virtually

## BED, AND BREAKFAST
### The Full Irish

everything at the last moment, which is a tough call for anyone to get right. If you find yourself in a situation where you are deep-frying the sausages because you can't cope with the pressure, then it's time to take stock of what you are doing. If you are under pressure, then hold the sausages and pudding, the tomatoes and mushrooms, and finish the bacon and eggs at the very end.

A fresh loaf of soda bread is perfect with the Irish breakfast, and some folk do also like to serve white bread toast. But consider what they do in Northern Ireland, where sliced and toasted soda farl and the local potato bread triangles – known as "fadge" – are the mainstay of the meal. Making your own potato cakes is an excellent USP that too few cooks bother to do, but look at our recipe and you will see how easy it is.

If you are using fadge bought from the shop, make sure that you do more than toast it: it really needs to be heated slowly in a frying pan so that the density is hot all the way through. In a perfect world, the fadge is fried last in a pan that is rich with buttery, bacony juices

And if it is a pot of tea that someone requests to go with the Irish breakfast – and tea cuts the fattiness of the meal better than coffee – then serve the peerless tea blends of Barry's of Cork. Staying at a townhouse in Dublin recently, I was offered a vast array of various teas, all of them blended in England, all of them inferior to the Cork blends. The excellent Java Republic coffees, roasted in Dublin, plus their luxurious range of teas, are also of exceptional quality and should be on your shopping list.

Belfasts's Ash Rowan is one of the deservedly legendary Belfast B&Bs whose reputation has been made from their splendiferous

## BED, AND BREAKFAST
### The Full Irish

breakfasts. Here is Sam and Evelyn's marvellous breakfast offer.

**ASH ROWAN, BELFAST, BREAKFAST MENU**

All dishes served with freshly squeezed orange juice. Help yourself to fresh fruit salad, grapefruit or cereals

1. Continental – Tipsy porridge – flavoured with Drambuie and cream, fresh fruit, homemade breads and preserves.

2. Ulster Fry – (not for the faint-hearted) Bacon, egg, mushrooms, tomato, white pudding, soda and potato bread

3. Just Bacon & Eggs - (for the faint-hearted)

4. Flambéed Mushrooms – Flambéed in sherry, flavoured with fresh cream and served on toast

5. Luxury Scramble – Scrambled eggs with strips of smoked salmon on toast

6. Irish Scramble – Scrambled eggs with chopped mushrooms, bacon served on potato bread

7. Vegetarian Scramble – Scrambled egg with mushrooms, tomato and cheese served on potato bread

8. Plain Scrambled Egg – Served on toast

9. Poached Eggs – Served on toast

10. Smoked Kippers – Pan-fried in butter and flavoured with rosemary

11. Kedgeree – Smoked haddock, eggs, rice combined with cream and hint of cumin, baked and served en cocotte

12. Tuna Fish Paté – Served with toast

**BED, AND BREAKFAST**
**breakfast bread**

## BREAD

I once gave a talk to a bunch of tourism MBA students in Dublin. Running through the nuts and bolts of what made for success in hospitality and tourism, I stressed that offering a freshly baked loaf of bread for breakfast was maybe the greatest USP any establishment could have.

One student was so shocked by my suggestion, she interrupted me straight away. "But, hang on," she said. "If you are going to have fresh bread, that means you have to get up early to bake it!"

This startling revelation, to an MBA student!, seemed to have arrived out of the ether with the force of a bullet. "You have to get up early to bake it!"

Well, yes, indeed you do have to get up early, and you don't need an MBA to figure that out. What you also need to do with breakfast is to consider how your breakfast can carry a freight of USPs (Unique Selling Points) that will make your breakfast celebrated and make your house or hotel a destination address. To put it simply, breakfast as a meal offers limitless possibilities, so long as you don't simply cook by rote. If you unleash the potential that lies in this most taken-for-granted feast, you can build your reputation on each and every detail of it. So, let's start with the staff of life: bread.

## "EVERY LOAF OF BREAD HAS A SOUL."

**DANIEL LEADER**

**BED, AND BREAKFAST**
breakfast bread

## SODA BREAD

Soda bread is the Irish bread, the single most important USP of the traditional Irish breakfast. The mixture of bread soda and buttermilk makes for a loaf that is singular and distinct, and delicious. It is also simple to make, and inexpensive, and you need to have your own version to serve at breakfast time.

The secret with soda bread is to leave it well alone: soda bread needs little work and a light hand. It is, truly, a loaf where the ingredients conspire together to do the magic, and your job is simply to shepherd it safely into the oven and then onto the table. Served when still slightly warm, this simple peasant loaf can offer one of the most unforgettably sublime taste experiences.

## THE TECHNIQUE

When he demonstrates his bread making technique, Ken Buggy, of Buggy's Glencairn Inn in West Waterford, first gives a list of necessities: "teaspoon, knife, flour, wooden spoon, bread soda, mixing bowl, buttermilk, oven on high, floured baking tray".

Gather together the above. Put one overfilled kitchen cup of white flour into the bowl, and add two heaped cups of brown flour. Sieve in one rounded teaspoon of bread soda (the soda is the only thing you sieve). Add three-quarters pint buttermilk. Whizz round with the wooden spoon as if constructing a roux. Lightly bring together the dough, finally using a little more white flour to seal it. Shape into a ball and place on baking tray. Cut deeply — nearly all the way through as it will heal together

## BED, AND BREAKFAST
### breakfast bread

— in the shape of a cross. Bake for 40 minutes and then rap on the bottom to ensure it is cooked: it should sound hollow.

Are there secrets to getting it right? Well, lightness of touch is perhaps the key – you don't knead the dough, and you should work quickly: soda bread should be made and in the oven in a trice. Serve it warm from the oven to enjoy it at its best.

> "BY THE SECOND HALF OF THE NINETEENTH CENTURY SODA BREAD HAD GAINED WIDESPREAD POPULARITY THROUGHOUT THE COUNTRY.
> THIS MAY IN PART BE ATTRIBUTED TO THE FACT THAT WHEN SODA IS COMBINED WITH SOUR MILK OR BUTTERMILK IT PRODUCES A VERY LIGHT AND PALATABLE LEAVENED WHEAT BREAD THAT COULD BE SUCCESSFULLY PRODUCED IN A DOMESTIC SETTING."
>
> **REGINA SEXTON AND CATHAL COWAN,**
> *IRELAND'S TRADITIONAL FOODS*

# BED, AND BREAKFAST
## breakfast bread

## THE PERFECT LOAF

Carmel Somers' Soda Bread is the one of the simplest soda breads we know of, with a rich, crumbly texture. You can see a full demonstration of it by Carmel, of West Cork's Good Things Café, on www.bridgestoneguides.com at the following url: http://www.bestofbridgestone.com/mb/ap3/ss.html

### CARMEL SOMERS' WHOLEMEAL SODA BREAD

700 g (1½ lb) stoneground flour (Carmel recommends Abbey Stoneground Flour)
225 g (8 oz) white flour
1 teaspoon salt
2 teaspoons bicarbonate of soda
2 eggs
75 ml (3 fl oz) olive oil
1 tablespoon honey
600-750 ml (1-1¼ pint) buttermilk
generous handful of seeds and grains (such as pumpkin seeds, sunflower seeds, wheat berries and wheatgerm)

**METHOD:** Grease two 450 g (1lb) loaf tins and preheat your oven to maximum.
• Mix together your flours. Add salt. Sift in the bread soda. Break the eggs into a separate bowl and whisk with the olive oil and honey. Stir the eggs into the flour. Stir in the buttermilk. Stir until you get a soft, moist, just pourable consistency.
• Add the seeds and grains. Press the dough into the tins, coming up to nearly the top. Put the tins into the oven (preheated to max). Cook for 20 minutes. Turn down the heat to approximately 180°C/350°F/mark 4 and cook for a further 30 minutes approximately.
• Check to see if the bread is done. Take out of the tins and tap the base to see if it makes a hollow sound.
• The finished loaves should be soft, crumbly and dotted with seeds.

## BED, AND BREAKFAST
breakfast bread

## FLAVOURED SODA BREAD

The Chocolate and Cherry soda bread is a recipe from Herb Quigley, baker extraordinaire, who will be remembered by many for the fine cooking he and his wife, Chris, produced when they ran Ballycormac House, in Tipperary. It was a recipe inspired by *pain au chocolat* in France: "The rich flaky pastry filled with bittersweet chocolate, and usually served warm, is a true taste treat. I had been making Irish soda bread for our breakfast table for some time and decided to play a little." Chris frequently uses this bread to make French toast. It can also be served with piles of streaky bacon cooked very crisp, American style.

"All measurements are in US cups, a simple measurement for bread making: you can buy a plastic measuring jug with cup measurements in just about any hardware shop. The dried cherries are worth hunting down, but if you can't get them, substitute dried apricots."

The Saffron and Sultana Soda Bread is a bright, golden delight of a thing, whose sunshine warmth makes the heart glad. It's an idea by Noel McMeel, chef at Monaghan's Castle Leslie.

> "BREAKFAST CAN BE THE DULLEST OF MEALS OR A REAL FEAST; IT ALL DEPENDS ON THE CARE WITH WHICH YOU SOURCE YOUR PRODUCE."
>
> **DARINA ALLEN**

# BED, AND BREAKFAST
## breakfast bread

### CHOCOLATE AND CHERRY SODA BREAD

3½ cups strong white flour

1 heaped teaspoon baking soda

1 teaspoon salt

4 tablespoons caster sugar

2 tablespoons butter

½ cup dried cherries

¼ cup chopped bittersweet chocolate or tiny chocolate chips

1½ cups buttermilk

**METHOD:** Sift together the flour, soda, salt and sugar. Cut in the butter until the mixture looks like fine crumbs. Stir in the fruit and chocolate and make a well in the centre. Pour in the buttermilk and mix until a light dough forms. It should look like thick porridge.
- Grease a 7-inch cake pan and pour in the dough; sprinkle with a little flour. Bake at 220°C/425°F/mark 7 for 10 minutes.
- Reduce the heat to 200°C/400°F/mark 6 and bake for 40-45 minutes.
- The bread is done when brown and sounds hollow when tapped on the bottom. Remove from the pan and wrap lightly in a tea towel to cool.

### SAFFRON AND SULTANA SODA BREAD

good pinch Saffron

568 ml (1 pint) buttermilk

450 g (1 lb) plain white flour

1 level teaspoon baking soda

salt

1 teaspoon sugar

120 g (4-6 oz) sultanas (sun-dried are recommended)

**METHOD:** Soak the saffron in the buttermilk overnight. Pre-heat the oven to max. Mix together the dry ingredients. (Sift the baking soda.)
- NB. Make sure you mix the sultanas right through the flour before you add the milk, because once you add the milk, you have to work quickly.
- Mix the milk with the flour to a wet consistency. Turn out of the bowl and shape with your hands on the board. Put onto a floured tray. Shape the cross with your finger.
- Bake for about half an hour.

**BED, AND BREAKFAST**
breakfast bread

## BOXTY AND POTATO BREADS

Boxty is Ireland's answer to the grated potato cake found in many cuisines, but it differs inasmuch as traditional boxty-in-the-pan uses the starch left-over after the grated potatoes have been squeezed in a tea towel to release their water. The water is poured off, and the grated potato is placed back in the starchy bowl, mixed with flour and salt and pepper, then formed into cakes and fried in the pan.

It's delicious, but it's also rather starchy for breakfast-time. So, we came up with something that we might call Boxty-Lite. This is how you make it: grate your potatoes and squeeze in a tea towel to rid them of water, then mix with salt and pepper and some melted butter: no starch or flour. Fry it in small cakes, made by adding two-tablespoons of potato mixture to a hot pan. When cooked, serve it with smoked salmon and sour cream, or with fried bacon and tomatoes. Or serve it as part of the Irish breakfast fry. It's boxty, but not quite as we know it: lighter, sharper, less filling, less starchy, a great breakfast treat.

You can customise the boxty by adding chopped parsley, or chopped chives, either of which will give it a lovely fleck of green colour and a fresher flavour.

You can make the boxty lighter again, if you decide to rinse the grated potatoes completely in fresh water, then squeeze out the water, and once again, mix with salt and pepper and melted butter. This is slightly more difficult to cook – the starch clinging to the potato helps to hold it together as it cooks in the pan – but the unrinsed version is truer in spirit to the great traditional Irish dish of boxty.

# BED, AND BREAKFAST

**FORTVIEW HOUSE, GOLEEN, WEST CORK, BREAKFAST MENU**

All of our juices are taken from freshly squeezed fruit

Orange Juice; Apple Juice; Grapefruit Juice
Fresh half Grapefruit
Carrot and Orange Juice; Carrot and Apple Juice

Orange, Mint and Grapefruit cocktail
Compote of fresh Orange segments and marmalade

•

Breakfast Fruit Salad (Prunes, Apricots, Banana and Raisins)
Porridge; Homemade Nut and Grain Muesli; Fruit Yoghurt
Cornflakes; Fresh Fruit muesli; Muesli

•

Homemade Pancakes and Maple Syrup
Local Farmhouse Cheese Plate
Hot Potato Cakes, Crème Fraiche and Smoked Salmon
Omelette
Kippers
Scrambled Eggs
Standard Irish Breakfast (bacon, egg, sausage, tomato, black and white pudding)
Poached Egg on Toast
Fresh Fish
Boiled Egg
Scrambled Eggs and Smoked Salmon
Fresh Fruit Plate
Banana topped with Yoghurt and sprinkled with Muesli
(Eggs are laid by our happy lazy hens)

•

Breakfast scones, Toast, Homemade Jam and Marmalade
Tea, Coffee, or Herbal Tea

Any Combination of the Above

# BED, AND BREAKFAST
**breakfast bread**

## CLASSIC BREAKFAST BREADS

"Get the pan on" is the urgent cry to Northern Irish mammies when their offspring return to home shores. The North has some fine craft bakeries whose specialisation in preserving the traditional breads – bannocks, soda farls, fadge, wholemeal breads – is especially gratifying. Here are some examples.

### BANNOCKS

175 g (6 oz) strong white flour
1 teaspoon salt
½ teaspoon bread soda
142 ml (5 fl oz) buttermilk
flour for dusting

**METHOD:** Sift the flour into a bowl with the bread soda and salt. Put a heavy griddle pan, or Le Creuset-style large heavy frying pan onto a low heat on top of the stove.
- Slowly add the buttermilk to the flour, pouring with one hand and kneading with the other. The mixture should gather together into a ball and come away from the sides of the bowl. Turn out onto a floured board and knead very lightly for a few seconds.
- Then, using a rolling pin, roll the flour out into as perfect a circle as you can manage by a combination of rolling and spinning the dough. The bread should be half an inch thick. Cut a cross into the circle, almost dividing it into four triangles. Lightly butter the, by now warm, frying pan with a little used butter paper, and place the circle of dough into the pan. Cook for approximately 20-30 minutes, turning after ten minutes.
- Watch the heat carefully; too high and the flour on the outside will burn, too low and the bread won't cook. Judge it by watching that the outside crisps and the bread rises slightly. Go for a cooler heat rather than risk burning the bread, you can always cook it for a few minutes longer if you feel it's still moist.
- This soda bread is usually served toasted. Bannock sandwiches are a treat. Split and toast a triangle and fill with bacon, sausage, onion and even a fried egg.

# BED, AND BREAKFAST
## breakfast bread

### FADGE

Fadge is the name given in certain parts of Northern Ireland to the revered potato cakes which are a treat served with an Irish breakfast. Make sure your cooked potato is quite dry for this bread.

350 g (12 oz) cold cooked potato (about three large spuds)
salt and pepper
50 g (2 oz) butter
50 g (2 oz) flour

**METHOD:** Always make the bread with cold potato otherwise the butter will melt and the mixture will be too floppy.
- This bread is ideal for using up leftover mashed potato, and especially flavoured potato purées (purées flavoured with parmesan or olive oil are much recommended, though not particularly Irish. Just make sure the purée isn't too wet).
- If you are preparing potato just for this bread then cook half or quarter pieces of potato in a little water. Drain into a mouli, or if you haven't got one of those, drain into a bowl and use a potato masher.
- Mash or purée your potato and while it is still hot, add the salt and pepper at this stage. If you want to flavour the bread with herbs or cheese, then this is the time to do it. But the true Irish fadge is not flavoured. Leave the potato to go completely cold.
- Mash room-temperature butter into the cold potato with a fork, pushing the prongs right through the spuds to distribute the butter evenly.
- Sift the flour into the mixture and, again using a fork, mix the three ingredients totally.
- With floured hands shape scoopfuls of potato into thin, flat oval pancakes. Cut across the central half of the pancake, giving you two heel shapes within the oval.
- Put your heaviest pan onto a low heat.
- Dust the breads with flour and cook for about 20-30 minutes. Play around with the heat so that it's hot enough to brown the bread, but not too hot so that it will burn the flour.
- Shake the pan so that the bread won't stick, and turn the bread at regular intervals.

# BED, AND BREAKFAST
## breakfast bread

### BREAKFAST PANCAKES

These pancakes are like English Drop Scones, rather than the American idea of a pancake. In Ulster they are often stuffed with potato and apple. They are eaten sweet, with jam or honey, or savoury, with an Ulster fry.

113 g (4 oz) flour
¼ teaspoon bread soda
1 tablespoon caster sugar
salt
1 egg
170 ml (6 fl oz) buttermilk

**METHOD:** Sift the dry ingredients into a bowl. Make a well in the centre.
- Beat the egg with the milk and pour it into the centre well of flour.
- Whip with a fork until the mixture turns to a smooth thick cream.
- Warm a heavy pan and smear it with some butter paper. The pan should be warm but the butter must not smoke.
- Take tablespoons of the batter and dollop them into the pan.
- When one side browns, flip over, using a palate knife. When the other side is brown the pancake is cooked.
- This makes about a half a dozen pancakes.

**BED, AND BREAKFAST**
working on the egg

## WORKING ON THE EGG

The first dish that alerted me to the brilliance of Richard Olney's classic cookery book, *Simple French Food*, was his dish of scrambled eggs with tomato and basil.

The dish is one of two recipes for scrambled eggs in a short chapter that includes recipes for omelettes and poached eggs, along with instructions on how to make the perfect hard-boiled egg, i.e. an egg that is neither hard nor boiled.

Aside from the exquisitely written instructions dealing with egg techniques that adorn every page of the chapter, the scrambled egg recipe seemed especially curious and imaginative. Olney's scramble aspires to a "creamy suavity", which seemed like some sort of culinary heaven worth chasing after: "Correctly prepared, the softest of barely perceptible curds held in a thickly liquid, smooth, creamy suspension, scrambled eggs number among the very great delicacies of the table", he writes.

Olney does it like this: he fries some peeled, seeded and chopped tomatoes with a little bouquet garni and some crushed garlic cloves and a pinch of sugar just until the tomatoes are coated with oil, then he discards the bouquet and the garlic. He puts two ounces of cubed butter with eight or ten eggs, beats them lightly, then puts them into the tomato mixture. His scrambling technique is to do things slowly, in a pan or a bain-marie, stirring all the while until the mixture begins to set.

Then, he adds in some basil leaves, chopped at the last second so they don't blacken, removes the eggs from the flame just before they are at the desired consistency, and keeps stirring. They are served straight away, of course.

# BED, AND BREAKFAST
## working on the egg

So, eggs and butter, slowly cooked together, will give you a scramble that is rich, suave, and which doesn't stick to the pan: this is of major importance!

What I like about this technique is the control it gives the cook. You can scramble eggs quite quickly this way, and you can also scramble them quite slowly, and by altering the heat you can be in control all the while.

What I also like is the texture. Because there is no cream or milk, and because the cooking is done slowly, the egg white never sets hard, so the dish has a mellifluous texture. You can eat these for breakfast with coffee, you can have them for brunch with a Bloody Mary, you can have them for supper with a glass of white wine. And the addition of the tomato and basil is inspired, giving the eggs an extra dimension of freshness and sweetness. Made with fresh, farm eggs, this is a dish to die for, an extraordinary piece of creative cooking.

So, it was scrambled eggs that tuned me into Richard Olney's way of cooking, but others have used egg cookery to propel themselves to fame. La Mere Poulard of Mont St Michel in northern France is perhaps the most famous egg cook of them all.

Madame Poulard cooked but a single menu day in, day out, year after year: omelette, ham, fried sole, pré-salé lamb cutlets with potatoes, roast chicken with salad and a dessert. But it was the lightness of her omelettes that made her celebrated throughout France, and indeed omelettes made in her style are still cooked in the town's restaurants to this day.

In 1932, Madame Poulard finally revealed her secret in a letter to a Monsieur Robert Viel:

## BED, AND BREAKFAST
### working on the egg

"Here is the recipe for the omelette: I break some good eggs in a bowl, I beat them well, I put a good lump of butter in the pan, I pour in the eggs and I stir them constantly. I am happy, monsieur, if this recipe pleases you."
Annette Poulard.

So, that is how you make a national and enduring reputation.

## "ALL FOOD IS THE GIFT OF THE GODS AND HAS SOMETHING OF THE MIRACULOUS, THE EGG NO LESS THAN THE TRUFFLE."

**SYBILLE BEDFORD**

Bill Granger, one of Sydney's hottest restaurateurs, made his reputation with… scrambled eggs. Granger's scrambled eggs were so famous that the *Sydney Morning Herald* placed them first on a list of definitive Sydney flavours. Like Madame Poulard's secret, Granger's recipe has no secret whatsoever: "Here it is – free-range eggs, a good non-stick pan, and lots of cream!", he writes in his book, *Sydney Food*.

If there is a secret to Granger's eggs, it is that he folds the eggs in on themselves as they set, almost like a cross between a scramble and a folded omelette.

It works a treat, but the cream does whiten the egg mixture, which I don't like so much: if you have healthy eggs with burnt-orange yolks, you want to show them off. It is also quite rich: a

## BED, AND BREAKFAST
### working on the egg

third of a cup of cream to two eggs creates a rich breakfast.

Working on the recipe, I came up with a formula that scrambled two eggs in a heaped teaspoon of butter in a pan, and then stirred a teaspoon of crème fraiche in at the last minute. The crème fraiche is lighter than cream, the reduced amount adds voluptuousness to the texture of the eggs without adding too much richness, and the acidity of the crème cuts that richness. The colour of the eggs is also left largely undiminished. A little sea salt and black pepper, and send it out.

We shall be looking at some more of Bill Granger's ideas later in this chapter, but anyone who is exhausted with the ritualistic cooking of breakfasts and gasping for new ideas and approaches should note that Granger's three books – *Sydney Food; Bill's Food* and *Bill's Open Kitchen* – each have a chapter devoted solely to breakfast ideas. Ideally, you will have all three books on your kitchen shelf.

## EGG IDEAS

• Scrambled eggs are delicious served with crisp white-bread croutons scattered on top: the contrast in textures is the key to the success of the dish.

• Scrambled eggs love freshly cut and chopped chives, stirred in at the end of cooking to preserve their allium freshness.

• Eggs en Cocotte: eggs bake beautifully with smoked salmon, or - if you have large beef tomatoes, slice off the top, hollow out the interior, season with salt, then crack an egg into the tomato pouch. Bake in a 200°C/400°F/mark 6 oven for 12-15 minutes, until the egg is just set. Sprinkle toasted breadcrumbs and chopped chives on top and serve.

• Quite the most luxurious egg breakfast we have encountered is Pio Cesare's

# BED, AND BREAKFAST
## working on the egg

Breakfast, as described by Antonio Carluccio. You make a bagna cauda by poaching garlic in milk, then stirring in some anchovies and, after the mixture is strained, adding some cream. Separate the whites from two eggs, then cook the whites in a pan in a little olive oil until just set, then add some of the bagna cauda. Plop in the yolks, and cook until they are just warm and runny. If you can possibly get it (or afford it!) you shave a little white truffle over the eggs just before serving. Truly voluptuous. Truly decadent.

• Paul Flynn, the acclaimed chef-proprietor of Dungarvan's The Tannery Restaurant, likes nothing better of a Sunday morning than a boiled egg and marmalade sandwich: spread some buttered toast with marmalade, spread soft-boiled eggs over, sprinkle with salt, place the sandwich together and eat with plenty of napkins. "I have told many friends about this ritual and my penchant for boiled egg and marmalade sandwiches and all of them, without exception, tell me I am a sick puppy," writes Mr Flynn in his book, *An Irish Adventure with Food*.

• Googoo Eggs. This is a great breakfast for children, and our kids were reared on it: shell soft-boiled eggs carefully, then place them in a cup (it has to be a cup as you will be holding it) with a knob of butter, and some sea salt and pepper. Chop roughly with a knife, and serve to the infant with a spoon.

• Poached Eggs. Bill Granger's tip on poaching eggs is this: Bring 5cm (2in) of water to the boil in a shallow frying pan. Turn off the heat and add the eggs at once. To minimise the spreading of the whites, break the eggs directly into the water, carefully opening the two halves of the shells at the water surface so that the eggs slide into the water. Cover the pan with a tight-fitting lid. Leave the eggs to cook undisturbed in the water for about 3 minutes. The eggs are cooked when the whites are opaque.

• Here is an idea for poached eggs from Elizabeth David: Have poached eggs prepared: melt some butter in a pan, slide the eggs in carefully, and sprinkle over some chopped herbs. Parsley, tarragon or chives or, best of all, a mixture of the three. Leave the eggs in the pan for a few minutes to warm through, basting with the butter and herbs, then squeeze a little lemon juice over them and serve.

• A frittata of egg, just cooked with a little sautéed tomato dice, and/or pancetta, will look very decorative when served in a half egg shell. With a little marinated anchovy, it also makes a great topping for an oyster! Two ideas from Moreno Cedroni of Italy's Ristorante Madonnina del Pescatore.

**BED, AND BREAKFAST**
fish

## FISH

Fish for breakfast is pure luxury, one of the quintessential treats – and one of the simplest treats. A fresh fillet fried specially for you, and ideally eaten in a country house dining room not a mile or more from a fishing port, or a fresh kedgeree or finnan haddie, is as good as it gets: simply add a squidge of lemon, a pot of Earl Grey tea, and some warm soda bread for ultimate yumsville.

## SMOKED SALMON

Irish smoked wild Atlantic salmon is one of the glories of Ireland's food culture, and one of the most glorious examples of how artisan skills and an extraordinary ingredient combine to produce an icon food.

To see this icon food at its best, try any one of the four smoked salmons made by the quartet of fish smokers who together constitute the first Irish Slow Food Presidia. The ISWAS (Irish Smoked Wild Atlantic Salmon) Presidia comprises Belvelly Smokehouse of Cobh, Woodcock Smokehouse of Castletownshend, Dunn's of Dublin and Ummera Smokehouse of Timoleague. These are peerless products, and of course they are expensive, as the wild fish is rare. But there are other quality smoked salmons to look out for: Kinvara organic smoked salmon is fine and very consistent, as is the salmon smoked in Connemara Smokehouse Ballyconneely; excellent smoked fish is also produced by Bill Casey's in Shanagarry; Lisdoonvarna Smokehouse in County Clare; Clarke's of Ballina in County Mayo and Shorescape Seafoods of Bandon in West Cork.

## BED, AND BREAKFAST
### fish

# SMOKED SALMON IDEAS

- To make smoked salmon and scrambled eggs really interesting, don't just serve a slice of cold smoked fish beside the eggs. Instead, use the trimmings of smoked salmon and, just as the eggs are finishing, stir in the strips of salmon. The heat from the eggs will cook the salmon very slightly, which gives an interesting piquancy to the dish.

- Leftover trimmings of smoked salmon also make baked eggs more interesting. Simply place pieces of smoked salmon in the bottom of a ramekin, pour over a little cream, then crack an egg on top. You can add another splash of cream on top, or maybe just a little knob of butter. Bake in the oven in a bain-marie – a large dish containing water that comes half-way up the ramekin – until the egg is just set, about 10-12 minutes.

- Take a classic menu idea from Eugene MacSweeney, formerly the chef-patron of Kilkenny's Lacken House. Mr MacSweeney used to serve some home-cured salmon with a colcannon potato pancake and a mustard and dill sauce. You can place a slice of smoked salmon on top of our boxty-in-the-pan, then use a mustard and dill sauce as a dressing, or something as simple as sour cream whisked with lemon juice to be drizzled over. The contrast between the hot boxty and the cold salmon is crucially delicious.

- In Ballycormac House, in Tipperary, Herb and Christine Quigley used to serve smoked salmon with a delicious rhubarb compote and spiced bread (see the recipe for the spiced bread in the Appendix). Here is our recipe for rhubarb compote to accompany smoked salmon:

### RHUBARB COMPOTE

700 g (1½ lb) rhubarb, cut into small pieces
50 g (2 oz) caster sugar

**METHOD:** Stir the sugar into the rhubarb, and leave in the bowl for 15 minutes, to draw out the rhubarb juices.
- Place in a saucepan and simmer, stirring occasionally, for ten minutes.
- Remove from the heat. Do not stir. Let the rhubarb cool overnight, when it will thicken. Store in the fridge, and serve cold with slices of smoked salmon and spiced bread.

## BED, AND BREAKFAST
**fish**

## SMOKED HADDOCK

This classic kedgeree recipe is from Joe Geoghegan, who cooked in the West Cork Hotel for many years. The very simple curry sauce is a marvellous foil for the rice and fish, and turns the dish into more of a brunch event. Use good smoked haddock such as that smoked by Frank Hederman or Sally Barnes for this: the nasty brown supermarket stuff will scuttle your best efforts.

**WEST CORK HOTEL KEDGEREE**

400 g (1 lb) smoked haddock (or you can use fresh salmon)
milk for poaching; bay leaf; lemon
3 hard boiled eggs
butter
100 g (4 oz) finely chopped onion
200 g (8 oz) long grain rice
250 mls ($1/2$ pint) water
25 g (1 oz) curry powder

Curry sauce:
250 mls ($1/2$ pint) cream; 25 g (1 oz) mild curry powder; 2 dessertspoons mango chutney
50 g (2 oz) fresh parsley

**METHOD:** Poach smoked haddock in milk with a bay leaf and a lemon and take out when cooked, about 5 minutes.
• Cook the eggs – place in a pan, cover with cold water, bring slowly to the boil, hold for a couple of minutes on heat, then cool immediately under cold running water.
• Melt a knob of butter in a deep pan.
• Cook onion without colouring for 2-3 minutes.

## BED, AND BREAKFAST
### fish

- Add the rice and cook for 2-3 minutes.
- Add the water and curry powder.
- Bring to the boil, and simmer for approximately 15-20 minutes. By this stage the rice should be cooked with not too much liquid left.
- While this is cooking make the curry sauce.
- Put all the ingredients into a thick bottomed pan and stir, bring to boil, then simmer gently while the rice is cooking.
- Flake the smoked haddock into the rice, add the freshly chopped parsley and stir in.
- Roughly chop the hard boiled egg and mix in lightly to the kedgeree and correct the seasoning.
- Serve in an oval dish with sprigs of fresh parsley and wedges of lemon, and the curry sauce in a sauce bowl.

Ken Buggy's breakfasts, as prepared in The Glencairn Inn, in West Waterford, are legendary, and the finest testament to their deliciousness which I can think of came from a French friend who stayed there some years back.

Our friend began breakfast with a selection of rollmops, ham and cheeses.

Then he ate some porridge, laced with Irish whiskey.

Then he had Finnan Haddie with poached eggs.

Then he ate a traditional fried breakfast.

Reader, he ate the lot.

I can only presume that he then was able to do little more than return to bed, but I'm not sure about that bit.

Here is Mr Buggy's recipe for the smoked fish, the Finan Haddie, with eggs.

"The question: how long do you cook Finnan haddie? is a bit like the question: how long is a piece of string?" says Mr Buggy. "Timings cannot be accurate and can only be based on personal taste. The simplicity of this dish only adds to the problems."

## BED, AND BREAKFAST
**fish**

What Mr Buggy likes about it is "that old-fashioned taste. It's got one of those smells you can taste: you smell it and you think: that's got to be Finnan Haddie. It makes me think of Christmas, home, the Aga, the open fire, that peaty, traditional taste."

### KEN BUGGY'S SMOKED HADDOCK WITH POACHED EGGS

Serves 4

450 g (1 lb) fillet of smoked haddock

milk to cover

pepper, salt, lemon juice, nutmeg (optional)

4 eggs

knob butter

handful chopped parsley

**METHOD:** Try to get the centre piece of the fillet of haddock as this is the best shape.
- Turn the oven to high.
- Wash and dry the haddock, then place in a small iron or glass casserole, so that the fish is comfy, i.e. a tight fit. Barely cover with milk.
- Season with plenty of pepper and a sprinkle of sea salt and a dash of lemon juice. You can add a pinch of nutmeg if you wish.
- Toss over a little bit of chopped parsley, add a big knob of butter.
- Cover the casserole, place into the centre of the oven and turn the heat down to medium.
- Cook for about 10 minutes. Remove from oven, and now gently crack 4 eggs over the haddock - you can crack them first onto a saucer and slide them in: it is important that the yolks do not break. Return to the oven. Cook for 5-7 minutes - this depends on how well you like your eggs done.
- To serve: take lid off, sprinkle with fresh parsley and place dish onto the centre of the table so people can help themselves.
- The egg yolks should run when you cut into them, says Mr Buggy. Why? Because it looks better.

## OFFAL

Leopold Bloom is not simply the hero of James Joyce's novel *Ulysses*, he deserves to be a hero to every food lover throughout the world. Endlessly musing on food, when he isn't actually eating it, Mr Bloom makes his first appearance in the novel in the act of making breakfast. Tea and bread and butter for Molly, milk for the cat, and suddenly the thought of kidneys enters his mind as he moves about the kitchen, and Bloom cannot get those kidneys out of his mind, so he walks down to Dlugacz's butcher's shop, and pays threepence for his kidney.

Back home, he drops it into a buttery pan, adding some pepper, then forgets about it and almost burns it, but then finally eats it with pleasure. Kidneys make a fine breakfast. At the Wall family's lovely Hanora's Cottage in Waterford, home to one of the greatest Irish breakfasts, here is what they do with kidneys:

**HANORA'S COTTAGE LAMB KIDNEYS IN GRAINY MUSTARD SAUCE**

4 lamb kidneys
butter, salt and freshly ground pepper
2 dessertspoons Irish wholegrain mustard
150 ml (¼ pint) cream

**METHOD:** Remove the skin and membrane from the kidneys and cut into bite-size pieces. Sauté in a little butter on the pan, turning occasionally until cooked, approximately five minutes, on a medium heat. Season with salt and freshly ground pepper. Add the cream and mustard, bring to the boil and simmer for three or four minutes until the sauce thickens slightly.
• Taste and correct seasoning, and serve immediately.

**BED, AND BREAKFAST**
**fruit**

## FRUIT

Fruits remain under-used in Irish breakfasts. Oranges get squeezed for juice, grapefruit may still get sprinkled with sugar and grilled, and pears may be poached, but too many addresses still don't get the attraction of fruit. There are a million Irish fruit salads out there that are not the best way to start the day.

This is partly understandable. The quality of fruit in Irish supermarkets is indifferent, at best, and many people haven't experienced the magic of a perfectly ripe apple, or a squidgy mango, or a pristine avocado. In some cases, a little searching will unearth a good Irish source – the beautiful apples grown by Con Traas of The Apple Farm, in County Tipperary, will blow you away the first time you try them. Think local: organic growers frequently have fresh fruits growing.

But, if the quality is not the greatest, then it needs some help, and that help is a sugar stock. Fruits poached in a sugar stock blossom with flavour: At the Ballymaloe Cookery School, one of the very first things students are shown how to make is a classic sugar stock, and it couldn't be simpler: a pound of sugar to a pint of water, dissolve the sugar in the water over a low heat, then boil for a couple of minutes. Now, you are ready to transform your fruit into masterly creations.

The other trick in transforming fruit is to roast it. Roasting intensifies the sugars, creating deliciousness in the oven. A very adult way to do this is first to fry your fruit in butter, then sprinkle with sugar and glaze it under the grill. Plums and peaches love this, also figs, and slices of apple. Pineapple can be grilled with great success, sharpening the sugars.

# BED, AND BREAKFAST
## fruit

## THE COMPOTE

Whilst we principally associate compotes with summer windfalls of fruit, they can be made very successfully with dried fruits. Hazel Bourke, of Assolas House in Kanturk, north Cork, makes the finest compotes we know, and here is Hazel's recipe for winter compote, using dried fruits. "The spices give the syrup a nice 'Christmassy' taste and smell!" she writes. All this needs is some good quality yoghurt, and you have achieved perfection.

### ASSOLAS HOUSE WINTER FRUIT COMPOTE

450 g (1 lb) mixed dried fruit (prunes, apricots, apple rings, figs and pears)
1 tablespoon Calvados (optional)
570 ml (1 pint) cold tea (approx.)
55 g (2 oz) sugar
2-3 whole cloves
5 cm (2 in) piece of cinnamon stick
1 star anise
pared rind of 1 orange

**METHOD:** Soak the fruit overnight in the Calvados and just enough cold tea to cover.
• Next day, transfer to a saucepan, add the sugar, spices and orange rind. Bring to the boil and simmer gently until the fruit is soft (or cover and put into the simmering oven of an Aga). It will take about 25 minutes for the fruit to soften.
• Remove the orange rind and spices before serving.
• This compote may be served hot or cold, and will keep very well in the fridge. Serves 4-6.

## BED, AND BREAKFAST
fruit

## RHUBARB

One morning we got a phone call out of the blue from a B&B keeper in the West of Ireland. "I've found a staggering combination, just by chance, and I want to patent it as my own. I don't want anyone copying the idea," she said.

And the combination? Rhubarb and Strawberry. The lady in question was devastated when we told her that this was one of the classic fruit combinations, already printed in many cookery books. But we could understand her excitement - when in season, rhubarb makes a fabulous fruit for a breakfast menu. Combine it with strawberry, or with some crystallised ginger, another classic.

We got the idea of adding grenadine to rhubarb from Con McLoughlin and Karen Austin from Lettercollum House. It restores any colour that may have been lost during cooking, and complements the flavour beautifully.

### RHUBARB & GRENADINE COMPOTE

450 g (1 lb) rhubarb
3 tablespoons water
3 tablespoons sugar
splash of Grenadine

**METHOD:** Slice the rhubarb, sprinkle with the water and sugar and place in a covered pot on a medium heat for about 6 minutes, until the rhubarb is soft, but not broken up.
• Very carefully stir in the Grenadine, being careful not to turn the whole thing into a stewy mess.

# BED, AND BREAKFAST

**POWERSFIELD HOUSE, DUNGARVAN**
**BREAKFAST MENU**

Freshly Squeezed Orange Juice

Freshly Squeezed Pink Grapefruit Juice

Cranberry Juice

Apple Juice

•

Greek-Style Yoghurt with Honey

Home-made Muesli with Rhubarb and Ginger

Peach Compote with Natural Yoghurt

Porridge with Cream and Honey

Selection of Cereals

•

Full Irish Breakfast

Field Mushrooms with lardons (if available)

Scrambled Eggs and Smoked Salmon

Grilled Bacon and Eggs

French Toast with Maple Syrup and Strawberries

•

Selection of Breads

Croissants, Banana Bread, Brown and White Scones, Toast

with a selection of Jams and Jellies

•

Tea, Coffee and Herbal Teas

**BED, AND BREAKFAST**
grains

## GRAINS: PORRIDGE AND MUESLI

Muesli, sometimes called Bircher Muesli after the Swiss doctor who first championed it in Zurich, should only contain raw natural ingredients, nothing refined. Typical ingredients are flaked oats mixed with grains, nuts and dried fruit. These can then be mixed again with fresh fruit, such as grated apple, or strawberry.

**APPLE MUESLI**

2 cups rolled oats
1 cup apple juice
2 cups grated apple
juice of 1 lemon

**METHOD:** Soak the oats overnight in the apple juice. Just before serving turn in the grated apple and lemon juice.
- Serve with yoghurt, honey and more fruit.

Toasted muesli, or granola is very easy to make and makes a sumptuous feast that belies the healthful origins of this superb breakfast treat.

Instead of butter and honey, you can vary the recipe using brown sugar and vegetable oil. We use a formula taken from Bill Granger's *Sydney Food* - three quarters cup honey, 125g butter, 500g rolled oats. And to this basic trio we add a whole host of grains, nuts and dried fruit. Below is a sample. But you can vary it easily by adding different fruit, such as dried blueberries, cranberries, different seeds, different nuts.

# BED, AND BREAKFAST
## grains

### TOASTED MUESLI/GRANOLA

¾ cup (6 fl oz) honey
125 g (4 oz) butter
1 teaspoon vanilla essence
500 g (1 lb) rolled oats
1 tablespoon sesame seeds
100 g (3 ½ oz) coconut flakes
1 cup rye flakes
1 cup spelt flakes
1 cup quinoa flakes
1 cup pumpkin seeds
½ cup sunflower seeds
1 cup flaked almonds
2 cups chopped dried fruit (such as apricot, fig, sultanas)

**METHOD:** Heat the oven to 190°C/375°F/mark 5.
- Put the honey and butter in a small saucepan and melt gently. Add the vanilla essence. Mix everything except the dried fruit in a large bowl and pour in the melted butter mixture. Stir with a large spoon until the grains are covered with the mixture.
- Turn out into a very large oven tray, or two medium trays, and bake in the preheated oven for half an hour, stirring every 10 minutes to keep the edges from browning and to distribute the butter and honey. (Be careful during the last 10 minutes – granola can burn easily.)
- Remove from the oven and add the chopped dried fruit. Cool and store in an airtight container.

# PORRIDGE

The food writer Philippa Davenport has described porridge as "the polenta of the Celts". A speciality of Cork's artisan food

## BED, AND BREAKFAST
### grains

culture is Donal Creedon's superlative Macroom oatmeal, roasted in the legendary Walton's Mill, in Macroom, Cork.

Here, working alone, Mr Creedon judges the roasting and toasting of the oats entirely by feel, smell and appearance as he moves the grain around on the kiln with the help of a large swing paddle. Mr Creedon's secret is his roasting of the oats, for this intensifies the flavour, giving smokiness and adding a nuttiness to the oats. Macroom Oatmeal takes a while longer to cook than normal oats, but the time is well spent: Macroom Oatmeal is one of Ireland's greatest treasure ingredients.

To elevate Macroom oatmeal from the splendid to the sublime, one needs to take another treasured Irish ingredient – Irish whiskey – and to stir in a capful of the booze when the steaming porridge is brought to the table. The heat burns off the alcohol, so it's not so hedonistic as it sounds, and it is the most wonderful fun. This practice is well established in Northern Ireland, in particular, where some of the best B&B's make a speciality of it. Elsewhere, we have seen people experiment by drizzling a necklace of rum around the steaming porridge.

### PORRIDGE IDEAS

- Porridge can be made from a mixture of grains. As well as the more usual oats, you can use rolled/flaked rye, wheat, spelt (an old variety of wheat which is low in gluten), or barley.

- A gluten-free porridge or muesli can be made from a basis of rolled rice.

- Other liqueurs which taste good with porridge are Drambuie and Irish Mist.

- Top porridge with some baked, caramelised fruit.

# BED, AND BREAKFAST

**KILGRANEY COUNTRY HOUSE, BAGENALSTOWN**
**BREAKFAST MENU**

Freshly Squeezed Orange Juice

•

Selection of Breakfast Cereals

Lightly Spiced Stewed Fruit and Yoghurt

Porridge with Jameson Irish Whiskey

•

Orange and Raisin Pancakes served with Crème Fraiche

•

Traditional Irish Breakfast with Bacon, Egg, Sausages, Clonakilty Black Pudding, Mushrooms and Grilled Tomato

or

Scrambled Eggs with Smoked Salmon

•

Tea or Coffee

# BED, AND BREAKFAST
à la carte

## THE À LA CARTE BREAKFAST

What happens if you don't want to do the conventional breakfast, with its range of fruit-cereals-eggs offer? What happens if the traditional breakfast simply doesn't suit the style of your address: if you are a cutting-edge place with funky punters, then you want something at breakfast time that is out-of-the-box. You need a new USP.

Consider, then, the à la carte breakfast, a series of choices where the guest can mix and match different elements to get just what they want. The à la carte works almost like a form of brunch: they might feel like tomatoes à la crème on toast, with some bacon curls on the side. Maybe a wedge of avocado on toast with some sautéed mushrooms with parsley. They might crave something sweet to begin – strawberries gratinated on toast – and then some farmhouse cheeses with coffee.

If they have travelled the globe, they might have a yen for a Japanese breakfast: miso soup; grilled salmon; pickled radishes; salted plums; green tea. Or you might be able to show your expertise with a Nordic-style breakfast buffet: crisp breads and flat breads; cured meats; herrings; an array of flavoured milks and flavoured yogurts.

In the search for a signature, don't limit yourself, and be prepared to think sideways when it comes to the first meal of the day. Or else, do limit yourself and do one thing – things on toast, for instance – superbly. Play to your strengths, but just don't let yourself get bored doing the same breakfast morning after morning. If you feel tired just thinking about doing it, then your guests will feel tired eating it.

# BED, AND BREAKFAST
## a la Carte

## À LA CARTE BREAKFAST IDEAS

• Things On Toast: Grill some sourdough, dribble with olive oil, top with ripe, sliced avocado, salt and freshly ground pepper. Serve with a Virgin Mary. Place some strawberries on slice of home-made white bread, sprinkle with sugar and place under the grill until the sugar begins to caramelise.

### OYSTERS ON TOAST

Oysters, as many as you like

25-40 g (1-1½ oz) unsalted butter, per 12 oysters

2 slices of bread, or more or less as desired

lemon wedges

**METHOD:** Open the oysters, reserving the liquor. Melt the butter in a frying pan and toss in the oysters.

• Stir-fry for no more than 40 seconds, depending on the size of the oysters. Do not overcook.

• Toast the bread. Using a slotted spoon, remove the oysters from the pan and pile them on to the toast.

• Pour the reserved oyster liquor into the pan, swilling it into the butter. Pour over the oysters. Add a lemon wedge.

• Tomatoes à la Crème. This can be served on toast or as a side dish. Slice the tomatoes in half, widthways. Melt some butter in the pan, and fry the tomatoes cut side up for five minutes, then turn and fry cut side down for another three-five minutes. With the tip of a sharp knife pierce the skin in five or six places, now turn the tomatoes cut side up and pour in some cream. Leave for a few more minutes to let the cream thicken. (Adapted from Edouard de Pomiane's recipe for Tomatoes à la Polonaise.)

• Good farmhouse cheeses for breakfast include thin slices of Coolea, wedges of Gubbeen or Durrus, because they are mild, and Boilie, the little golf balls of goat's cheese. Tipperary's Baylough is also a favourite choice of Irish B&Bs.

• Bacon Curls, an idea from the great Bill Granger who suggests you twist slices of bacon into circular "curls" and then roast them in the oven. They keep their shape whilst cooking.

• Mushrooms make a great side dish, either sautéed with garlic and parsley, or, if you have a large field mushroom, then roasted in the oven.

## BED, AND BREAKFAST
the mood

### SETTING THE BREAKFAST MOOD

There are certain things that enrage me when I am staying in hotels, B&B's or country houses: an indifferent greeting; bad housekeeping; sloppy service. But nothing enrages me so much as when I come down for breakfast, take a seat, orientate myself to the room, begin to make up my mind as to what I want to eat, and, then, it hits me: they are playing the radio on the music system. *AA Roadwatch. Morning Ireland. The Today Programme. Classic FM. The Full Irish.*

Listen, if I want the Full Irish, I want it on a plate. I don't want it in the form of gossipy low-brow entertainment drizzling from the speakers. And I don't want to hear of the troubles besetting the world as I attempt to enjoy my breakfast. Even if it is early and I am due out fast to go to a meeting. I want breakfast to give me a respite: I want the meal to set me up for the morning. I don't want the troubles of the planet to intrude on someone's efforts to cook and serve something special.

Perhaps so many places play the radio at breakfast time because they reckon that people do actually want to listen to news and traffic reports, and maybe they are right.

But, if they are right, they are correct at the expense of the mood of the room: after all, do the retired couple having a mid-week break want to hear of the traffic jams in Loughrea? That is relevant to people driving to Galway, but it is inimical to the mood you should be setting for those people staying with you who are taking time off.

Perhaps another factor in playing the radio is simply people's fear of playing the wrong sort of music at breakfast time. I

## BED, AND BREAKFAST
### the mood

stayed in a country house in County Kerry recently, where a selection of classic opera arias was the featured soundtrack: you know, a snip of *Aida*, then a whack of *Carmen*, then the duet from *The Pearl Fishers*. If they had played *Tristan und Isolde* all morning I could have stomached it, but this was a truly dyspeptic musical mélange.

If certain music destroys mood, then certain music succeeds superbly in creating mood. I always remember having an early morning cup of coffee in Belfast's smart shop, Equinox, in their café. The pleasure to be enjoyed wasn't just from the Rosenthal coffee cups, or the luxuriously funky chairs and tables. No, the best bit was the gloriously mellifluous Mozart piano concertos flowing and ebbing in all their glory in the ether.

Superbly rhythmic, superbly pleasing and, consequently, superbly relaxing, the experience taught me that getting the music right meant getting the mood right: for the space of ten minutes Equinox gave all of us there a little idyll, an oasis of contentment as we enjoyed a breakfast bite.

Does this mean you need only rush out and get a boxed set of the Mozart piano concertos? Well, that may be simplistic, but it's not a bad place to start. Add in a boxed set of J.S. Bach – choose Murray Perahia's versions of much of Bach's keyboard works, as an example, or the glorious versions of the piano music by Angela Hewitt – and you will have hours of music that you cannot tire of.

But there is very much Early Music that can also set a mood perfectly: with Hildegard von Bingen I am happy as a sandboy, ditto with any recordings by the vocal group, Anonymous 4. And, if in doubt, remember that silence can be golden.

# TESTIMONY

**Catherine Fulvio, Ballyknocken House & Cookery School, Wicklow**

Having grown up in the hospitality business, in my experience the key to success in hospitality is:

For your guest to enjoy a first-hand experience in a second-hand business. Interestingly, in a business that recycles bedrooms, linen, tables, chairs and crockery, there are satisfied customers who are willing to pay good prices for this service. The reason being that the successful provider is giving a first-hand experience, whereby the guest is treated like a king (or queen).

How to give a first-hand experience in hospitality

## 1. LOVE YOUR JOB

Guests will always feel and appreciate your enthusiasm.

## 2. UNDERSTAND THE NEEDS OF YOUR GUEST

The dictionary explains HOLIDAY as follows:
"A time of intermission or rest. Freedom from work or cares. Leisure time for contemplation."
Rest, freedom from cares, leisure…. Your guests reasoning for taking a break. What you have to do is not only meet these needs, but reach beyond expectations.

## 3. REACH BEYOND EXPECTATIONS

Let's not forget the high standards in our guests' own homes nowadays. To impress, you need to better this.

## 4. COMFORT BEYOND EXPECTATIONS

I refer not only to comfort in bedroom facilities but also warmth of atmosphere. Firstly a personal warm welcome is of ultimate importance. Thereafter, actual warmth through attentive and discreet service, log fires, candles, pleasing music, attractive furnishings and fittings and areas of your property for relaxation and contemplation.

## 5. FACILITIES BEYOND EXPECTATIONS

I recently found the first Ballyknocken House brochure, printed in 1969 when we were charging 21 shillings for B&B and we advertised "all modern facilities such as hot and cold water"! Well, it was modern then! Your property's facilities must be above the guest's expectations, well presented and all in good working order. You can enhance your facilities e.g. offer local walks, tie in with local golf clubs or gardens.
Strangely, many guests ask prior to booking "what is there to do?" Yet, upon arrival, they sink into a comfort zone by simply relaxing

# TESTIMONY

and enjoying their surroundings. A guest with no experience of your property fears that he/she may be bored. In reality once you meet all their needs for comfort, they really just want to rest (see point 2).

## 6. FOOD BEYOND EXPECTATIONS

The key to everyone's heart and surely one of the most talked about subjects. A disappointing meal is a story often repeated. You do not need that kind of publicity! Good food is not about extensive choice but about top quality. It is better to provide less from high quality fresh ingredients, well cooked and presented than to offer a big menu of mediocre food.

## 7. BE CONSISTENT

Now that you have set your high standards, you must remain consistent and striving only to improve.

## 8. ADD YOUR PERSONAL TOUCH

The guest will always appreciate your personal touch, whether it is tea and scones on arrival or taking that extra bit of time to chat about the local attractions.

## 9. HAVE AN ELEMENT OF UNIQUENESS

Do try to offer something that your competitors are not offering, whether it is a typical local dish on your breakfast menu, a special wine collection, a package to include beginners fly-fishing... something to capture the imagination of your potential guest.

## 10. MARKETING & FINANCE

When you feel you have your product and pricing right, tell people. Word of mouth is the most valuable marketing tool. Existing customers return and also encourage friends and colleagues too. This costs you nothing. Publicity and critical reviews help, as this is an independent assessment of your product. A brochure and more importantly, a website are keys to attracting new business. Do make sure that you have good photographs of your premises in order to present your premises to the potential guest.

Media advertising is the last marketing tool as it costs you money! But it can be very effective if well targeted.

Much as you love the business, don't forget to make a profit! I remember sitting at a meeting between a hotelier and a banker. The banker asked what the hotelier expected from his business. The hotelier said, "to DELIGHT the customer", to which the banker replied, "I was hoping that you were going to say to make a PROFIT"! The answer probably lies somewhere between both, but you need to make a profit to reward your efforts and for reinvesting. And finally, after all of your hard work, don't forget to take a HOLIDAY yourself! Be somebody else's guest!

## BED, AND BREAKFAST
primer

# primer

- **The B&B business is a curious halfway house in hospitality: seemingly domestic, it is nevertheless a professional relationship. To make it work, you need to strike the right balance between these two demands.**

- **Generosity of spirit is what people using B&Bs want to discover. Whilst the relationship is a professional one, what they really want is to be treated like one of the family.**

- **Making a bed is not a straightforward task. Great, special, comfortable beds should aim to be somewhere between a shrine and a grotto, and you must work hard to make them special.**

- **A successful Irish breakfast is based on Irish artisan quality pork products. Without these, you are lost. With them, half the battle is won.**

- **With an Irish breakfast, timing is everything. If you find yourself deep-frying the sausages, it's time to switch careers to something easier.**

## BED, AND BREAKFAST
### primer

- Baking fresh bread in the morning is the greatest USP of them all. But you must work to create other USPs that will make the reputation of your breakfast. Madame Poulard did it with the omelette; Bill Granger did it with scrambled eggs.

- Always use the great icon foods of Ireland to best effect: smoked salmon; porridge; teas; black and white puddings; specialist breads.

- Assimilate the best ideas of the continental-style breakfast and give them your own signature style.

- Smart hotels cook the easier-to-manage brunch at weekends rather than the standard Irish Sunday lunch.

- If you are fed up cooking the standard Irish breakfast, then consider an à la carte breakfast, which features the things you like to cook and the dishes that let you shine.

- Consider the mood you want to set at breakfast time, and don't just switch the radio on without thinking about mood.

# 4

# THE HOUSE IN THE COUNTRY

# 4

"It's what the guests say as they swing out of the drive that counts."

ANONYMOUS, NEW YORK TIMES, 1947

# THE HOUSE IN THE COUNTRY

A rather quaint belief has existed for some years now which suggests that running a country house is a genteel pursuit, something which amateurs, who happen to have a big old pile out in the country, can turn their hand to with ease.

Rather like working in the wine trade, or running an antiquarian bookshop, inviting guests to come and stay in your place, some folk believe, is less of a job, more of a grand hobby in which you meet nice people and make a few bob to help with the costs of keeping the roof intact.

Forget it. The age of the amateur is over, if it ever existed. Hospitality is a business for professionals, and none more so than the endlessly intricate business of running a country house. If you have made a pile in banking or building call centres, and think running a country house is a nice way to pass your autumnal days, you will soon find that in fact it is perhaps the most demanding task of all in the hospitality game, a task that demands vocational levels of commitment.

The reason why it is so difficult is because you are not simply selling people a service, as you might do with an hotel or even a B&B. What you are selling is an experience, an out-of-the-norm experience, a nostalgic experience, a wannabe experience, a good-life experience. And, if all you do is provide a bed, dinner and breakfast, it isn't enough.

Let me explain it this way. I recently had a very annoyed country house owner on the telephone one morning, annoyed that they were no longer included in the *Bridgestone 100 Best Places to Stay in Ireland*, a book into which their lovely house, and its more-than-lovely gardens, had happily nestled ever since

# THE HOUSE IN THE COUNTRY
## out • of • time

I had first come across the house.

"But now," I explained, "you are no longer offering dinner, so I had no choice but to take you out of the book."

"But there are restaurants nearby, and if people ask, then I can prepare them a plate of smoked salmon or a salad."

"That's not dinner, and people who have travelled don't want to get back in the car and drive to a strange restaurant."

"But what about Place X, up the road? He doesn't do dinner!"

"But he runs a B&B. You are a country house."

"Why should that make a difference?"

"Because people's expectations are different. The country house guest expects dinner. The person staying in a B&B doesn't have the same presumption."

And suddenly the penny dropped. The annoyed country house owner suddenly realised that what they offer, what they have to offer, is a different, a qualitatively different, experience from a B&B.

This doesn't mean that the experience has to be a grand, 5-star, Big House Weekend experience. It simply means that it has to be of a piece.

For example, very many people who arrive at Myrtle Allen's legendary, and deservedly legendary, Ballymaloe House, in Shanagarry, east Cork, express bewilderment that this iconic address, the most famous address in Irish hospitality, should be so simple, so modest, so unassuming, so devoid of the trappings of other globally famous destinations. No top-dollar spa. No plasma televisions in the rooms: in fact, no televisions in the rooms at all! No hordes of liveried staff.

But what there is, is the Ballymaloe experience, an experience

# THE HOUSE IN THE COUNTRY
out • of • time

which is restrained, simple, elemental, and all of a piece, and just exactly what Myrtle Allen wants it to be.

If you get it – and it must be admitted that some people simply don't get it – then it is one of the most magical experiences you can enjoy in hospitality, because the combination of elements – the food, the rooms, the location, the art, the service, the ambience – is simply transcendent.

Ballymaloe gives you Ballymaloe, and that is what others cannot give you. Offering the standard 5-star stuff would, paradoxically, dilute the experience. Doing things the Ballymaloe way – simply, modestly, carefully, unchangingly – is the USP of this icon address.

The same is true of another celebrated, though much less well-known address, Frank and Rosemary Kennan's Roundwood House, in County Laois. Roundwood is simple, very simple, and one could be very critical of certain elements of the place. But, is anyone ever critical of the plumbing or the plasterwork? Of course not. And why not?

Because these elements all disappear because Roundwood offers people a perfect piece of the country house experience: bonhomie, great hospitality; lovely country cooking, a relaxed ambience, interesting guests, a charming sense of away-from-it-all, a step back in time.

The same thing happens in Temple House, in Ballymote, County Sligo, thanks to the instinctive hospitality of Sandy and Deb Perceval, thanks to the grandeur of this great house, thanks to Mr Perceval's endlessly-young bonhomie and sense of fun.

When you ratchet up the experience somewhat, and you offer people the experience of staying and eating in a castle, you must

# THE HOUSE IN THE COUNTRY
## out • of • time

aim for the same transcendence. Sadly, few addresses manage this with the necessary style and skill. Ballynahinch Castle, in Connemara, is one of the exceptions, and Ballynahinch succeeds for a simple reason: it may be a castle, it may be grand, but it is egalitarian.

Locals will be in the bar alongside high roller tourists from the 'States and Europe. The staff are local, the atmosphere is serene and joyful, the sense of place is total. The guests are all sorts of people from all sorts of places, but there is no sense of status being exercised, and it is precisely this sense of conferring status on wealthy guests that makes other castles less of a success: they are stuffy places, who think guests have to be pampered and spoilt and treated with kid gloves, rather than be entertained, and this very act makes them precious and self-conscious and, in my opinion, places that are fundamentally ersatz: Las Vegas castles, castles in the air.

The secret of a successful country house experience is trueness and transcendence: the guest is not simply paying for some time-out, they are buying into a piece of magic, the good life, the country life of claret and good cheer, vegetables from the garden, maybe even dancing in the pub, listening to musicians after dinner, or else sitting by a roaring fire quaffing snifters of brandy.

Be it only for one night, they want to believe that they are, in fact, someone else, in a time other than now. That is what the country house experience is all about, and if you can't achieve it, then you will not survive as a destination.

So, what makes the demands of the country house just so tough?

## THE HOUSE IN THE COUNTRY
out • of • time

The answer is that the focus is always on you: owner; host; chef; sommelier; raconteur; provocateur; guide; expert; calm and collected from early morning to last thing at night, an unquenchable provider of good times, of transcendence. That is one mighty set of demands, and some people aren't up to it.

I stayed in a very beautiful country house recently, owned by a couple who had made their money in the City and who had bought a very fine house and gardens and who were steadily withdrawing from their commercial lives to be country house hosts. Fine, except that whilst the house was comfortable and the cooking was good, there was simply no magic.

And there was no magic simply because there was no instinct for hospitality. They were doing something they thought they might like, they were, in effect, acting like hobbyists, but hobbyists don't cut the mustard when it comes to making an experience transcendent, because they don't have the magic, the instinct; they don't, above all, have the extraordinary generosity which running a country house demands.

If you want to run a country house, be prepared to give totally of yourself, your time, your life. If you aren't prepared to do that, stay in the City and increase your fortune.

> "THE QUALITY OF EGGS DEPENDS MUCH UPON THE FOOD GIVEN TO THE HEN."
>
> **ISABELLA BEETON**

## THE HOUSE IN THE COUNTRY
out • of • time

# primer

- In order to be successful, the country house experience must offer to the guest an experience where all the elements of the offer are of a piece: no discordancies.

- Simply offering a nice bed in a nice house with dinner isn't enough: the country house experience must allow guests to embrace the good life in a fundamentally nostalgic way.

- The best country houses offer guests an experience that is, cumulatively, transcendent. If you aren't achieving that, then no amount of top-dollar investment in facilities will make the experience happen.

- The secret of country houses is down to the people who run them: amateurs need not apply, for running a successful country house is one of the most demanding parts of the hospitality profession.

- Running a country house demands your all.

# TESTIMONY

**Patrick O'Flaherty, Ballynahinch Castle, Connemara**

## 1. KNOW YOUR PEOPLE

Nothing in a hotel operation is more important than the people who run it. This becomes more critical the more full service the operation. Ballynahinch Castle is a beautiful hotel with a great setting but without the dedicated people it is just one of many such properties in Ireland. The entire culture of your operation needs to be driven from a personnel perspective because, either directly or indirectly, that is what your customers are buying. This is a huge area, covering everything from recruitment to retirement.

## 2. KNOW WHAT YOU ARE TRYING TO ACHIEVE

Identifying your product and being true to it is of great importance. Do not try to be the answer to all things in hotels. It most likely will not work and will result in a lot of guests only getting half of any one experience.

## 3. BE CONSISTENT

One of the cornerstones of quality, consistency is of paramount importance. If you hope for repeat business, whatever it is you deliver, it must be there time and again. Just as importantly, this also applies when managing your team. They need to have confidence in their boss and know what to expect.

## 4. CONSTANT ENHANCEMENT

You cannot afford to go stale. Resting on one's laurels is a sure way to kill them. Identify the factors that work and keep them up to date and fresh. Change for change's sake is not necessarily a good thing. The old maxim, "if it works, don't fix it" applies. However, it is essential that the product keeps ahead or at least in pace with developing trends and attitudes.

## 5. WALK BEFORE YOU RUN

If you intend being around for a while then the evolution of your hotel needs to be an on-going process. However, if you make an improvement or addition to the service then only do it if you can do it without damaging the rest of your delivery. Then deliver it time and again until ready to further improve or adapt.

## 6. WATCH YOUR SALES

Amazingly many successful hotels seem to get complacent. It is as if the efforts made to

# TESTIMONY

become successful are no longer necessary once they get there. Commercial urgency should be a constant state. Nothing rises faster than costs when sales go soft; never take commercial success for granted or confuse critical acclaim with financial success.

## 7. VALUE FOR MONEY

The other cornerstone of quality. Your guests should leave your hotel saying, "What a great hotel" not "What a great hotel, ouch! A bit expensive." The cost is unimportant (within reason) as long as it is value for money. This is not a matter of whether or not a guest can afford to pay your prices, it is whether or not they are prepared to.

## 8. LISTEN

Knowing how to listen is essential. There are three people you need to listen to: your guests, your staff and yourself. Most likely in that order. Your guests will tell you soon enough if things are not right and your staff will send the message that they are not happy. You need to diagnose the problem correctly and decide if it really is a problem. Sometimes you may decide, no! This is not a valid comment; I am sticking to my guns.

## 9. GO OUT & TASTE

Other people have good ideas as well and you need to know them. You are not the only genius on this planet and if you do not keep abreast of what's happening and experience something a little different you will go stale. You should always be able to be impressed.

## 10. TAKE TIME OFF

Holiday, outside your work style.
Try to do something completely different to your work and in this way exercise and rest both your mind and body in a way that you usually do not, or at least do not do often. Otherwise you will be in danger of losing your perspective, making poor decisions and generally getting stressed.

# "A SMILING FACE IS HALF THE MEAL."

**LATVIAN PROVERB**

# 5

# HOTELS AND HOW TO RUN THEM

# 5

"Some people's food always tastes better than others, even if they are cooking the same dish...
because one person has much more life in them – more fire, more vitality, more guts – than others."

**ROSA LEWIS**

# HOTELS AND HOW TO RUN THEM

The calendar year 2003 presented me with a series of by-now-familiar values to be discovered in Irish hotels.

At the start of the year, working in County Clare, there was the hotel with the million-dollar location overlooking the lake, whose rooms were elegantly decorated with all the latest design ideas and colour schemes from 1950's Ireland. In particular, this particular address boasted a carpet that was amongst the most curious, and memorable, I have ever encountered.

The next morning, having checked out, I asked a friend who lived nearby, and who is one of the leading figures in Irish food, quite how one managed to achieve such an extraordinary uniqueness with a carpet.

"Forty years of cigarette smoke and spilt beer, and no proper cleaning," he explained.

My notes of the night's stay summarised the hotel in two words: "tragic & smelly".

I was back in County Clare at a major tourist destination during a bank holiday weekend, and managed to squeeze into an otherwise packed hotel. The only concern expressed by any member of staff regarding my comfort at this destination was when they told me my credit card had been declined as it had reached its limit, and did I have another card they could swipe.

Otherwise, they remained mute, and I left with the memory of dreadful service and the fact that there are still hotels where they think you make grapefruit surprise by opening catering tins of grapefruit segments in syrup.

In Dublin, at a highly-priced and newly opened hotel, at breakfast time I encountered some scrambled eggs whose texture really had to be seen and felt to be believed. Pale white, oozing

# HOTELS AND HOW TO RUN THEM
## twenty • four • seven

milk, formed into the shape of a large ramekin, they were brought to the table with a flourish by the waiter.

You could look at these "eggs", you could touch them, but you certainly couldn't eat them. No matter. The waiter returned after a few minutes, saw my lined up knife and fork on the plate, and took the plate away, again with an impressive flourish.

He didn't bother to ask why I hadn't touched the dish, or could he get me something else. He didn't care. His job was to ferry food, not to see if I was happy. If I had a complaint, that was the manager's job, not his. But, critics shouldn't complain, I believe, so I paid my whacking great bill and left.

Later in the year, breakfast in a hotel near to Galway was so atrocious that I broke my own rule: I complained.

"Was everything all right?" asked a lady at reception who I would guess was not just the receptionist, but also the owner. For once, I said, "Well, frankly, no, it wasn't" and I then went on to tell her that despite the presence of two waitresses in the dining room, every table that had been used by guests had remained uncleared, the buffet table had never been replenished, and my Irish breakfast would have failed to secure satisfaction from a canine guest.

"I write about Irish food and hospitality, and such an experience makes me feel ashamed," I said.

The good lady took the full cost of bed and breakfast and offered me my credit card slip to sign.

When this sort of thing happens, you tend to think you have reached the nadir. It can't get worse. It couldn't possibly get worse. Could it?

It sure could.

# HOTELS AND HOW TO RUN THEM
twenty • four • seven

It is late in the evening, late in the year, in County Cork, and I have a reservation for dinner and a room. I park the car, walk through the entrance doors, and there is no one at the reception desk. After a couple of minutes, a waitress appears with a couple in tow. She crosses behind the desk without acknowledging me, begins to punch figures into a credit card machine, then asks the couple; "Were there any drinks with that?"

"Yes, a bottle of house wine," replies the lady.

Transaction completed, the waitress turns to me.

"I have a reservation for dinner and a room. McKenna?"

"Oh. Okay." She consults neither reservations book nor computer, but simply says: "Follow me."

We walk through dining rooms, where there are a couple of tables of diners, past the loos, through doors and down a long corridor. Some of the doors of the rooms are open, so I can see that a number of the rooms are not made up, even though it is almost 8pm.

The waitress stops at one door, an unpainted fire door, and pushes it open. She switches on the light, and I notice that the light switch she pushes is actually cracked down the middle.

"There you go," she says, and I walk into the room.

Of the four lights in the ceiling, two are not working. The light over the bathroom sink is not working. The light over the desk is not working. The drawer of the desk is stuffed with papers, which turn out to be old menus and flyers. The television is not properly tuned. There are framed prints resting on the floor, tilted against the walls. Some of the other prints are actually hanging on the wall.

I decide to do the old "Let's dare to look under the bed" routine.

# HOTELS AND HOW TO RUN THEM
## twenty • four • seven

Under the bed, there are dust balls, scraps of paper, scraps of this and that. I decide to stop before I come across a piece of paper saying: "This bed is the property of Tracey Emin."

You might wonder when this part of the room was last cleaned, but without carbon dating it is unlikely you would have much chance of getting an accurate date.

I grab my bag, switch off the light at the broken light switch, close the unpainted fire door, and walk back down the corridor, past the unmade-up rooms, past the loos at the end of the dining room, through the dining room and back to reception.

There is no member of staff anywhere along the way to ask me why I am carrying my bag and haven't taken my coat off, given that I have a reservation for dinner. There is no member of staff at the reception, so there is no one to whom I can explain that it is simply impossible for me to stay and, as for the thought of having dinner…

In the car, I call a restaurant that also offers accommodation. "I'm sorry to be calling so late but I'm on the road and I wonder is there any chance I could book a room and dinner?"

"Sure, come in and we'll look after you," purrs the lady who answers the telephone.

And they did look after me. Saved by hospitality.

That word hospitality is important. My *Concise Oxford Dictionary* defines hospitality as: "Friendly and generous reception of guests or strangers".

But I saw no friendliness, and certainly no generosity, in these dreadful places. But when I did find it, I found it in abundance. What happens to allow people running hotels to sink to such appalling standards, or to be content with such low standards

## HOTELS AND HOW TO RUN THEM
twenty • four • seven

even when the hotel is smart, expensive and newly opened?

What are the regulatory or licensing authorities looking for when they award their ratings? Is there no regard for standards of service, hygiene or competence? What I encountered was incompetence on a gross scale, from businesses that were happily dealing with the public, though one can be certain that the public weren't so happy dealing with them.

There is another way of running hotels, a way which exemplifies and personifies that definition of hospitality: "Friendly and generous reception of guests or strangers." The Brook Lodge Inn, in Macreddin village, County Wicklow, was created by the Doyle brothers from a green-field site, and has quickly won a reputation for being at the cutting edge of creative, innovative hospitality.

The Killarney Park Hotel is one of two hotels owned by Padraig and Janet Treacy, and is one of those hotels that personify the virtues of the traditional, grand hotel.

Here is how these hoteliers do it.

## RETRO-INNOVATION:
## THE BROOK LODGE INN

The Brook Lodge Inn has many USPs: Unique Selling Points.

It is one hour's drive from Donnybrook Church on the southside of Dublin, a major consideration for weekend guests who don't want to drive for hours to get to and from a destination.

## HOTELS AND HOW TO RUN THEM
### twenty • four • seven

It uses only organically produced and wild foods in its menus.

It features an extensive Farmers' Market once a month, and twice a month during the summer.

It has a series of stand-alone shops, including a pub, on the grounds of the hotel.

It has an unconsecrated church on the grounds that can be used by wedding couples to have a blessing as part of their wedding reception.

It is a genuinely multi-functional campus: private guests; wedding guests; conference guests; spa guests; locals; tourists; business folk; all these can be found in the hotel on an average day.

All of these USPs are important, but I think that perhaps the most important USP of the Brook Lodge Inn is its philosophy of Retro-Innovation. That is to say: the best of the old with the best of the new, side by side.

You can see this in the design of both the exterior and interior: the exterior already looks comfortable and settled, after less than five years, thanks to a modest style of building that was mindful of scale, and which felt no need to be a modernist piece of architecture.

The interior synthesises various styles with winning aplomb: the clubby, wooded bar: the discreet reception area; the grand, low-key comfort of the lounge; the smoky, mirrored romanticism of the dining rooms with their reflective ceilings. It feels like a country house hotel, yet it isn't a country house, but it does have all the facilities of an hotel.

The cooking in the Strawberry Tree restaurant is sophisticated but in a rustic way that is true to the provenance of the

# HOTELS AND HOW TO RUN THEM
twenty • four • seven

ingredients and true to the seasons: in winter they serve winter food; in summer, they serve summer cooking.

The food may be grown and reared organically, in a pre-industrial way, but the style of presentation is right up-to-the-minute.

And the new parts of the operation have been cherry-picked to service the needs of a busy hotel: slick computer systems allow the front desk to know instantly the likes and dislikes of a guest when they make a booking. The grand new suites have plasma screens for television and computer technology. The kitchen can finish breakfast on a Sunday morning and effortlessly slip into gear to cook for upwards of a thousand lunchtime guests when the Sunday markets are in full swing.

The spa offers state-of-the-art treatments. The hotel is marketed with all the sophistication and effectiveness that modern marketing methods can achieve.

In other words, everything that can be used to make the experience of a guest as real, as true and as genuine as possible, is exploited. The experience of staying in the Brook Lodge Inn has the tactility and rusticity of an ageless country experience, but ultra-modern systems are used to ensure that the experience can be delivered satisfactorily for every guest, whatever their demands.

I have used the phrase retro-innovation as coined by the late Lionel Poilane, France's most famous baker. M. Poilane was famous for the huge wheels of sourdough bread baked in his little bakery and shop on the Rue Cherche Midi.

However, he also operated a bakery at Bievres, outside Paris, where 24 ovens produced 7,000 sourdough loaves a day, using

# HOTELS AND HOW TO RUN THEM
## twenty • four • seven

traditional methods. Innovation helps you to up the scale, whilst the tradition within which you innovate ensures the authenticity. Evan Doyle has been in catering all his working life. His brother Eoin has always worked in marketing, whilst Bernard Doyle works in property.

Evan Doyle had introduced his signature trademark of cooking with wild and organic foods whilst running the original Strawberry Tree Restaurant, on Plunkett Street in Killarney. He became convinced that Killarney could profit greatly from having the entire centre of the town pedestrianised, a move that he hoped would also benefit his restaurant and bar.

"The town should be for people, for tourists," he says. They succeeded in having the town pedestrianised for a month, during which every trader's turnover increased: "We had a fashion show along the middle of the street, we had food on the street, it was fantastic."

The experiment was discontinued, however, and it was whilst having a chat with his brothers one evening, and expressing his disappointment that the town hadn't gone ahead with the plan to close the town to traffic, that Eoin Doyle suggested that "it would be great to find an old village somewhere that was run down", where one could create a small hotel, renovate the pub, have some shops, and "have a village where people would want to go. And that's where it germinated from. It went on from there."

One Good Friday, the three brothers scoured the countryside looking for "somewhere off the beaten path, somewhere with a river, somewhere with a bridge, in a valley. They were the criteria." Bernard Doyle found a farm for sale in Macreddin with

# HOTELS AND HOW TO RUN THEM
twenty • four • seven

127 acres. Close to Aughrim village in the heart of County Wicklow, Macreddin had that stream, that bridge, and the comfort of gently sloping valley fields

Evan Doyle was also conscious that the site should be close enough to a major city in order that the hotel would not be affected by the winter downturn in the tourist season.

The foundation for the new concept remained firmly focused on the offer of wild and organic foods that Mr Doyle had introduced in Killarney: "The idea of having a restaurant with bedrooms was very appealing. The idea of having a country house hotel, but with a restaurant and not just a dining room was even more appealing. And we knew there had to be an attraction to Dublin not just for the leisure and pleasure, but for the corporate and conference market as well. They are the two markets we went after and still go after. Both home-based, both coming mainly from Dublin."

Monday to Friday in the Brook Lodge is corporate and conference, before the hotel swings around on Friday for the leisure and pleasure guests.

## "EVERYTHING IS ACHIEVABLE, WITH DIFFICULTY."

Evan Doyle admits that mixing these diverse groups with their diverse demands is "very difficult. But it is achievable. Everything is achievable, with difficulty."

The mantra of the Brook Lodge is that it is the individual guests "who need the pampering. If they feel they are second

## HOTELS AND HOW TO RUN THEM
### twenty • four • seven

place, there is trouble the next morning, and that is what you are trying to avoid. So, with the big wedding party or the big conference, you know you can rock it out, but it is those six couples who are here at the same time, or those twelve couples, you have to make sure that they know that you are on top of the case, that you know who they are and what they want, and that they are getting it."

Mr Doyle asserts that it is these private guests who have individual needs. "With the wedding or the conference, they have broad needs. The host or hostess is throwing a party, they have decided on the menu, they have decided on the food for their guests, so the guests are at the whim of the host and hostess. And you have had a chance to pre-empt that: you know what you are doing food wise, you know what you are doing service-wise, what you are doing wine-wise. But you don't know what these two people here want. And if you let them know that you are interested in finding out what they want, well, then you've won."

The marketing of the Brook Lodge to the corporate and conference sector is the responsibility of Eoin Doyle, whilst for Evan Doyle, "my job is, when they come in that front door, to make sure that in the time from when they come in that front door to the time they leave that they are looked after, both with food and drink and service-wise. That's what I do. That's what I have always done. The only difference is that there are bedrooms now, so it's twenty-four hours a day. That was a rude awakening!"

One of the factors that has aided Mr Doyle in coming to terms

# HOTELS AND HOW TO RUN THEM
twenty • four • seven

with his "rude awakening" has been the creation of a crew at the Brook Lodge during the first four years. "The skills I have here in the management crew have increased dramatically. Staff and management retention is very high, and that makes it a lot easier for me."

Mr Doyle stresses that individual staff members have "ownership" of their zone of responsibility: the equestrian manager has ownership of the equestrian part of the business, just as the girl behind the bar in the lounge has ownership of that room when she is on duty. To develop the Wells Spa, opened at the end of 2003, Mr Doyle has brought in a partner. "I come from food and drink and latterly bedrooms and hospitality. That facility out there: I can't run that. So, we have brought in a partner to run that."

Evan Doyle recognises that even though the Brook Lodge met with both commercial and critical success almost from the very beginning, it took approximately two years before he was completely successful in creating a crew "with whom I was in touch with every day, so that we are all going at the same pace and in the same direction."

Simple things such as the fact that most male staff in management don't wear ties, or that first names are used "and that all staff are at the same level" has taken time to inculcate, even though these are significant elements of the hotel's aesthetic.

"There is a successful formula with the crew here, so that staff know that if they are under pressure, they can ask any other member to help them out. There is no hierarchy. And there is a huge respect gained then, on both sides. I have been in too many

## HOTELS AND HOW TO RUN THEM
twenty • four • seven

hotels where the bar is busy and the duty manager helps out, and they don't know how to operate the till! And they're asking a member of staff: 'Where's the brandy?' I would hate that!"

## FEEL-GOOD FACTOR

Having varied elements to the hotel's offer has allowed a broad range of customers to gain access to the hotel. Locals who first visited the pub have become customers of the Strawberry Tree restaurant. Crowds who come for the Sunday markets are "people who you might never see at a country house hotel. It's all Feel-Good Factor. And anything we do here has to be Feel-Good Factor. That's what the market is. That's what the pub is. The Orchard Café is Feel-Good Factor. That's what it really is all about. If we have a function down at the church at nighttime, I will have candles all the way down the steps and across the bridge and hanging from the trees. That's what gives people a buzz. I just want to see people smiling and saying: 'Wow!'"

## THE CLASSICAL WAY:
## THE KILLARNEY PARK HOTEL

Padraig Treacy was born into the hotel business: his parents ran The Ross Hotel in Killarney, though it was not until he was in his mid-twenties, and following stints in the motor industry and other ventures, that Mr Treacy returned home to take up the

# HOTELS AND HOW TO RUN THEM
twenty • four • seven

reins of the business. Back home, he met his wife, Janet, who was working in hotel management. Other family members are also involved in the hospitality business in the town and in Cork city.

During the 1980's, the Treacys took the Ross to a position where "it was working like a Swiss watch, there was nothing else that could be done with it", so Mr Treacy went looking for a site to start a new venture.

By chance, they found the vacant site in the centre of town where they would be able to build the Killarney Park, "I had a vision of this hotel, like The Old Ground, in Ennis. I had been there once or twice and I liked the feel of it: in town, but still in its own grounds, and catering for residents, mainly. And we wanted to take it up a notch. My philosophy would be that if you are going to do a thing, do it right. And for our own sakes, we wanted to do it."

BES funding allowed the project to begin at what was, economically, an unprepossessing time for any new tourism venture. The hotel opened in 1992.

The KP has been characterised by an insistent striving for standards, which ultimately led to the hotel moving up from 4-star to 5-star rating under the guidance of an outstanding manager, Donagh Davern. Chasing new targets and goals seems to be the backbone of the Killarney Park. Mr Treacy sums it up in one of Donagh Davern's favourite shorthand expressions: "C.I.: Continuous Improvement. If the job can be done, it can be done better, and keep at it."

Where others have star ratings, and generally fail to live up to them in many and various ways, The KP is a shining example of

## HOTELS AND HOW TO RUN THEM
twenty • four • seven

# "I'M A GREAT BELIEVER THAT THERE IS NO SUCH THING AS BAD STAFF. THERE IS ONLY BAD MANAGEMENT."

**PADRAIG TREACY**

having every aspect of a huge, 90-room, 90-staff operation which is all of a 5-star piece, from food to spa rooms, from service to housekeeping, from check-in to check-out, from public spaces to private rooms, from bar food to breakfast. The only word that can describe it is: fastidious.

"I believe in standards. If you are going to do a 2-star hotel, it should be the best 2-star hotel. I'm not snobbish about this. Hostels, for example, have a role to play, and they should be there, but they should be the best."

"It just went right from the beginning," says Mr Treacy, "There was a 'can do, will do, must do' attitude, and we have people working here now who were here on the first day. Like Donagh, I would have the philosophy of working with people, I was reared to be looking after people. But we didn't see it as a means to an end, a way of taking money off people. It wasn't commercial. It was just that that was what you were supposed to do."

Whilst Padraig Treacy is unwilling to use the term "vocation" for the hospitality business, he asserts that "You have to love it,

# HOTELS AND HOW TO RUN THEM
twenty • four • seven

and you have to do it to the best of your ability. And this attitude of, 'Oh, it'll do'. Well, that won't do."

"I'm a great believer that there is no such thing as bad staff. There is only bad management," asserts Mr Treacy. "There can be an attitude amongst hotel owners that we are entitled to something. Well, we are entitled to nothing, until we do it." This level-headed, almost folksy approach means that management in the KP help out in the bar, heft luggage when needs be, and adopt a flat-system of working that avoids the old hotel hierarchy.

The desire to move from a 4-star rating to a 5-star arose because "our customers were demanding it, our staff were demanding it. It wasn't an ego trip for me. I would have been happy to be a top 4 rather than bottom 5." With Donagh Davern driving the improvements, the move upwards was achieved within 12 months.

The Treacys have continued to run The Ross, which they are now proposing to develop. "I work the tables there, and I love it, because that's where I was born", and the development will see it re-emerge as a 30-bed hotel of 4-star status. "The intention is we are going to take the food up a notch, but to keep the level of service, with friendliness rather than intrusiveness, and professionalism as well."

"The Ross has always been very lucky," says Padraig Treacy "It was a clean, well-run, decent place, and that does come through. You can't buy that. That's why I would be upbeat, and I would be very upbeat. We've been so lucky. We've had great luck. People say to me, 'How's it going?' and I say, 'Marvellous!' And I have to say, it's a lovely life."

# primer

- **Levels of complacency and poor service in Irish hotels are frequently shocking to experience, with a lazy, laissez-faire attitude evident in many places, regardless of whether they are budget accommodation or top-dollar destinations.**

- **Hospitality demands friendliness and generosity: can you look at your operation and be happy that you and your staff are delivering both?**

- **Thinking out of the box is rare in hotels, but it can deliver radical success if you have a vision of what you want to achieve.**

- **Every hotel needs to create an entire series of USPs if it is to succeed, from food to service to the very look and feel of the place.**

- **Retro-Innovate: take the best of the old and mix it with the best of the new.**

- **In hotels, everything is achievable, with difficulty.**

**HOTELS AND HOW TO RUN THEM**
twenty • four • seven

# primer

- **Private guests in hotels must never be sacrificed, in terms of attention paid, to corporate guests.**

- **Always aim to have your corporate guests return as private guests.**

- **There is no such thing as bad staff. There is only bad management.**

- **Every hotel must market its offer to a carefully selected target audience.**

- **Creating a Feel Good Factor creates something that is priceless.**

- **Continuous improvement should be the motto of every hotel, no matter how many stars it has or how famous it is.**

- **Standards are standards: if you have a 2-star place, then aim to make it the best 2-star place in the business. Likewise if you are a 5-star place.**

# TESTIMONY

Adriaan Bartels, Sheen Falls Lodge, Kenmare, County Kerry

## Ten things you need to know to succeed in hospitality...

**1.**
A sense of humour is a great help and will pull you through on the darkest days.

**2.**
You need to be persistent and have stamina.

**3.**
The busier the hotel the more buzz you get. It's a natural high.

**4.**
You must be able to pre-empt the guests' needs. You must never forget that guests can be unpredictable – expect the unexpected. This is what it is all about – a job that is different every day. You will never get bored.

**5.**
You need to be a diplomat, a democrat, an autocrat, an acrobat and a doormat.

**6.**
Every guest (staff member) wants attention more than anything else. Most complaints arise from guests (staff members) not having been given enough attention. Deal with complaints on the spot. Always say yes.

**7.**
The world is a small place – everyone who comes into the hotel is connected in some way to someone who uses/talks/or who will talk about the hotel. Never underestimate the guest, particularly those who just wander in off the street - they could be your future residents.

**8.**
No matter how happy you keep the staff (ultimately if the staff are happy, they will keep the guests happy) never assume that they will be with you forever. Staff always talk about guests – make sure the guests are out of earshot.

**9.**
Owners always raise the bar every year. Respect this and it will make life easy. However, this is difficult to do!

**10.**
Awards and industry recognition are great for the hotel and the staff – go for them!

**11.**
Always remember there are more than ten things you need to know to succeed in hospitality!

# 6

**RESTAURANTS WITH ROOMS**

# 6

"The proprietor was agreeable. His wine was good. There seemed to be evidence of care and conscientious innkeeping.... the beds were comfortable, the water was hot, the proprietor and his young wife were making a great effort to compensate with welcoming service and decent cooking for the unfortunate situation of their auberge."

**ELIZABETH DAVID, DESCRIBING A HAPPY DESTINATION IN AN UNLIKELY PLACE,** *AN OMELETTE AND A GLASS OF WINE*

# RESTAURANTS WITH ROOMS
welcome • comfort • cheer

The quotation from Elizabeth David's essay, *Eating in Provincial France 1965-1977,* at the start of this chapter, underlines one of the key elements of the Restaurant with Rooms: it can be a silk purse in a sow's ear.

Elizabeth David probably expected the worst from the little auberge set back only a metre from the main-Bordeaux-Paris autoroute. She had already had a lousy lunch, and indeed the essay is mainly about how disappointing the quality of food and service became over the 12 years the essay covers. But, she got a surprise, and "We left at daylight feeling, as travellers should, that we had been welcomed, comforted and cheered on our way."

This is how the RwR can work its magic. Because people's expectations are not high regarding the level of accommodation, the cook can concentrate on knocking people's socks off with superb cooking.

But there are other vital elements with a RwR:

If you want to run a restaurant in the country, away from the major population centres, you need rooms. Rooms mean people stay overnight: if they stay, you make money while they sleep. You also make money because they will have more to drink, so the average spend will increase, probably significantly.

And, for a young couple setting out in business, a RwR means you can get away with a small spend on the rooms. In country houses people expect grandness. In hotels their expectations are increasingly demanding.

But the RwR will succeed simply by offering simple rooms, which need no more than a shower, and by keeping the focus on food. So, the aesthetic of the RwR can be ascetic, and still

# RESTAURANTS WITH ROOMS
### welcome • comfort • cheer

succeed to a huge scale. Simple rooms also mean less housekeeping, so the couple setting out in business have no need to employ anyone else. Breakfast, likewise, can be a simple affair: many of the customers may well have to be gone early in the morning, needing to get back to work and families having snatched a night away from the daily grind.

There is another advantage for the RwR: the low cost of staying means that customers can become regulars: the harassed parents of young children who just need a night away when granny babysits and who desperately need some quality time together; the young lovers with stars in their eyes and almost-empty pockets; the stressed business-folk who need to get out of the city, even if they do need to be up at 7am next morning to get back to the grind.

But if the feeling and perception of value for staying overnight is very strong, and the memory of superb eating is still paramount, then all these people will return, time and again. Of course, they will most likely also always want to stay in the same room, people being people. That's not a problem: it's a positive.

The RwR will also have a local audience, who simply want to use the restaurant on its own, and who don't need the accommodation. But having that second audience – country houses don't have drop-in diners, by and large – gives you more business, more cashflow, and gives you an audience who will embed you in the community.

Simple rooms, a simple lounge where people can have a drink, and superb food: that is the trinity of demands of the RwR, and it is a trinity that can make decent money for the owners, simply because the customers pay to stay, and thereby have a bigger

# RESTAURANTS WITH ROOMS
welcome • comfort • cheer

spend at dinner. For people in hospitality who want to have freehold, in a world where that is becoming increasingly rare, the RwR allows you to be your own boss, in your own place. That is a nice feeling.

But, the downside is, if your cooking isn't up to scratch, then you won't succeed. The RwR is a Restaurant, with Rooms, and not Rooms, with a Restaurant. The cooking is paramount, and the cooking must stand alone: it must be the USP, the focus for the traveller, the focus for the local diner. Everything else is simply an add-on that allows the owners to make some more money in order to make the business flow more sweetly.

And what the menu must offer, then, is local foods. The menu must be a road map of the region. For the city person, the food must take them into the country where they are staying. It must not simply be an echo of the sort of thing they can eat every day in city places. Foods and wines should be different, distinct, idiosyncratic: local cheeses; local meats and game; wines from yet-to-be-discovered producers whom you have sourced with care; all of these things must be used so that you offer a taste of the region.

The RwR means that young people can make a living in hospitality without working for the bank, and without the sort of pressures banks exert on those with an overdraft or a bank loan. The RwR is the open-door to success. It is a very focused concept: you pay attention to the food, whilst the customers carry their own bags, and if you deliver on the food and deliver on the value, then you will have a regular clientele who are back every fortnight to grab some quality time and some quality food. The RwR is simple, very simple, and beautiful.

**RESTAURANTS WITH ROOMS**
welcome • comfort • cheer

# primer

- Always remember that a Restaurant with Rooms is not Rooms with a Restaurant: the cooking is paramount.

- A RwR must have a local audience, who only make use of the restaurant, along with the overnight guests.

- Don't be afraid to make breakfast a simple affair, otherwise you will wind up working all the hours.

- The value perception with a RwR is vital: simple rooms should carry a low price tag. The increased income will come from a bigger customer spend, whilst the value perception means customers will become regulars.

- A RwR must offer a menu that is a road map of the region: exploit the local specialities.

- If the cooking isn't up to scratch in a RwR, you won't succeed in creating a destination.

# TESTIMONY

Donagh Davern, Lecturer, Department of Languages, Tourism & Sports Studies, Waterford Institute of Technology

## Ten suggested key points towards the success of a hotel manager...

• The core concept of Marketing is to make products/services available which, satisfy customers' needs and wants. Relationship Marketing is essential for success - it's a lot easier to keep and nurture your existing clients than to find new ones. It's also a lot less expensive!

• Use your Guest History to record frequent guests' preferences in terms of favourite rooms, music, foods, drinks, etc. Then "delight" them by anticipating their needs on their next stay - allocate their favourite room; have their favourite CD playing in their room or a bottle of their preferred wine in their room.

• Take care of your guest's children - today's ten-year old is tomorrow's customer! Know their names, record them in Guest History, have their favourite chocolates in the room on arrival, have smaller bathrobes made for them, recognise their birthdays with a celebration. If the children like your hotel enough, they will always convince their parents to stay there!

• Spend time "on the floor" with your staff…what better way to find out what customers want and what your staff's challenges are? Empower your staff. Let them make customer service decisions, recognise guests' birthdays, anniversaries or other special occasions. Let them solve problems themselves, but always be there if they need help.

• 5-Star service doesn't need to be stuffy….provide 5 Star standards in a friendly and welcoming atmosphere. Make your guests feel comfortable…..Neat dress is fine in most restaurants. Draw the line at shorts and baseball hats, but why make guests wear a jacket and tie?.....who's paying the bill?

• Work for an owner that re-invests in their product, or better still own and reinvest in your own product! Constantly look out for the latest innovations and the next trend that you can put in place to "delight" your guests.

• Build a good rapport with your neighbouring hotels. Yes, they are your competitors, but there will always be

# TESTIMONY

opportunities to get each other out of a bind!

- Set goals for your hotel in terms of quality; strive to be the best operator in your market. Awards are a good goal to focus the attention of your staff. Should you receive an award, reward your staff – why not hold a special luncheon where the Managers serve the line staff?

- Create your own PR - let your guests know about renovations you have completed, awards you have received, and new additions to the management team, etc.

It's worth doing a press release, the newspapers might just run it for free!

- Surround yourself with colleagues who are forward thinkers and are full of energy.

- Pursue niche markets - don't try to be all things to all people. Choose your niche markets and provide special services and facilities to attract and serve these niche market customers, e.g. for the golf market provide printed directions to popular courses, early breakfasts, a drying room for golf bags and wet clothing, golf towels with your logo in their rooms, etc.

"MY PERSONAL PRIZE FOR THE CREATION OF KITSCH IN THE KITCHEN GOES TO A FIRM OF CATERERS IN THE NETHERLANDS WHO ONCE SERVED ME CHICKEN BREAST GARNISHED WITH A SLICE OF BRIE CHEESE, ACCOMPANIED BY SAUERKRAUT MIXED WITH MANGOES AND LYCHEES!"

**STEPHEN MENNELL**

# THE ART OF DESIGN

# 7

"The idea that an inanimate object can change your humour, affect your mood, is fantastic – the room that calms, enchants or excites you."

**JOHN ROCHA**

# THE ART OF DESIGN

Good design works in two ways:
1. You don't notice it, but it feels good.
2. You do notice it, and it feels good.

Bad design also works in two ways:
1. You don't notice it, but it doesn't feel right.
2. You do notice it, and it doesn't feel right.

Design and design consciousness has been the mantra of much of hospitality during the last fifteen years. Design conscious addresses – and they are not just hotels, but often also country houses and, on rare occasions, B&B's – have garnered not just miles of newspaper and magazine columns, but also entire books all to themselves.

Being in the hottest address meant being in the newest design concept: what Starck has been doing in New York and wherever; what Schrager has been doing here there and everywhere; what's happening in Miami; Dublin's riposte with boutique hotels; the hippest place in Stockholm, or Barbados, or the newest Christina Ong.

Is the Hempel still hot, or is it, at least, still cool? Is the Banyan Tree where the celebs still hang out, or have they moved on to Amansara or are they to be found eating Ferran Adria's cooking in Hacienda Benazazu?

Where on earth was it all going to end? The answer was always obvious: "We are tired of suffering for their art", wrote the editors of the quirky and hip Nota Bene travel guides at the end of 2003. "Although we applaud outstanding design, when it comes to hotels, we say: service and comfort first."

# THE ART OF DESIGN
### suffering • for • art

What?! Not hip, or cutting-edge, or super-cool, or far out? Not post-modern, or ironic? Not mega-buck, or celebrity designer? Comfort! Service! Those old guys!

The editors even went on to say that the design hotels seemed to employ staff "based on looks and hauteur rather than experience and ideals".

Experience! Ideals! Those old guys!

"What could once be classed as innovation...has become a cliché," they lament.

Experience. Ideals. Service. Comfort. What a strange quartet of wishes from the modern traveller in our self-conscious century. All that old stuff. And anyway: what has that quartet of wishes got to do with good design?

Simple. Good design creates comfort. Good design facilitates service, and thereby helps the staff express both their experience and ideals, because it lets them achieve their best, their optimum efficiency, their ideal of customer satisfaction.

But isn't one traveller's comfort another traveller's chintz and carpets? Surely it is impossible to please everyone with design? I don't believe it is impossible, though it is certainly difficult.

Good design is always of a piece, and it is always demonstrably thought-through, and it always has a signature. That signature can be classic – think Assolas Country House in north Cork or Fermoyle Lodge in Connemara or Dublin's Clarence Hotel. It can be funky – think Coast Townhouse in Tramore or The Morrison in Dublin or Kilgraney in County Carlow. It can be serene – think Newport House in Mayo, or The Mustard Seed in Limerick or The Killarney Park Hotel. It can be quixotic – think Shelburne Lodge in Kenmare or Kerry's

## THE ART OF DESIGN
suffering • for • art

Iskeroon or Dolphin Beach near Clifden.

But whatever it is, it needs demonstrably to have been considered: colours, textures, furniture, fabrics.

That doesn't mean that it needs to cost a great deal of money. Some of the least comfortable places to stay in Ireland are also amongst the most expensively fitted out: heaven save us from the 5-star hotel where the designer has been given a multi-thousand-euro budget for each room. When that happens, you get overkill, and overkill is not comfortable, because it is not serene, quixotic, classic or funky. It is simply unimaginative, and an enormous waste of money.

The rule is: don't think cost. Instead, simply think. Imagination is the key to successful design; that and suitability. Every great piece of design is, essentially, a synthesis of influences, a synthesis of preferences, a synthesis of accords: the right thing in the right place where it not only looks right, but feels right, and works right.

Getting that result leads to what we might call good feng shui, and by feng shui I mean something that engenders a feeling of comfort in the guest. Feng shui is tactile, welcoming, comfortable, colourful, restrained, appropriate, intuitive, something that is satisfying to the eye and the senses, something that feels, looks and works just right.

Feng shui is destroyed by careless thinking: the desk in the wrong place; the light that doesn't work at the right height; the wrong colour of towel – I recently stayed in a smart little hotel in Germany, and my room had a luxurious big bathroom in black and white tiles. Unfortunately, the black and white tiled bathroom was furnished with pinky-orange towels. Aargh!

# THE ART OF DESIGN
## suffering • for • art

It is ruined when form and function don't unite, when design becomes gratuitous. Many country houses, for instance, have bad feng shui simply because they are cluttered with inherited furniture that the owners are unwilling to sell. If you have heirlooms, keep them in your own space, and don't inflict them on guests: if they look wrong and feel wrong, they are wrong, and just because they have been in the family for decades won't make them feel right or look right.

But many hotels over the last decade have also allowed their design to be gratuitous: they wanted you to suffer for their art. Chairs might have looked smart from a distance, but when you sat on them, there was no support, no comfort. Colours used could be shocking and aggressive, because some design crew said this was what was fashionable. Shocking and aggressive is, simply, shocking and aggressive: it's never fashionable.

If you can't achieve this effect of functioning, aesthetic design on your own, then call a friend. One of the most successful design collaborations in Ireland in recent years was the collaboration between Maeve Coakley, owner of Kinsale's Blindgate House, and the interior designer Beatrice Blake. Blindgate wasn't a big budget project, but the fusing of the imaginations of these two women resulted in a subtle, successful house with its very own aesthetic. Something similar happened in Kelly's Resort Hotel, in the collaboration with the painter Guggi, whose simple bowl shapes were used as part of the signature decoration of the room as well as on the crockery of Beaches Restaurant, in the hotel.

And that is what good design should be aiming at: a distinct aesthetic, a look and a feel that is unique, and specific to the

## THE ART OF DESIGN
suffering • for • art

building, whether you are a two hundred bed hotel or a two bed B&B, whether you are time-worn country house or the simple but sparkling rooms in a restaurant with rooms.

It goes without saying – though we do have to say it, because so many people forget it – that great design will always be undone by poor housekeeping. You must make everything gleam, because you cannot create a wow! factor unless the appearance of your premises is pristine.

When things glisten and gleam, then people notice them, and take pleasure from them. If they don't glisten and gleam, then all that people notice is the grime, and you can take it as read that people will not come back a second time to see if you have cleaned the place up. Good housekeeping is also good maintenance, and good maintenance cuts down on costs in the long term.

Comfort. Service. Ideals. Experience. When you are designing, never forget all that old stuff. Great design facilitates all that old stuff, and makes it vivid and real.

## TESTIMONY

**Shelagh Conway, Marble Hall, Dublin**

- Display friendliness.
- Maintain top-quality product.
- Watch pricing levels.
- Be informative to guests - go out of way to help - a holistic approach is essential.
- Demonstrate home cooking ability - structure proper menus - give wide choice.
- Avoid over-intrusion - give people space.
- Monitor competition.
- Network with other providers in suitable geographical areas.
- Be aware - maintain links with appropriate organisations in the hospitality industry.
- Be active locally.

## THE ART OF DESIGN
suffering • for • art

# primer

- Don't be a slave to design. If your chosen scheme doesn't work, all that people will ever notice about it is that it doesn't work.

- Successful design demands intense consideration, whatever your budget. Simply throwing money at a design scheme is simply throwing money away: a high spend won't disguise a lack of imagination.

- Your aim with design is to create excellent feng shui: form, function, comfort, beauty.

- Great design creates a signature style, so don't be afraid to be different.

- If you can't do it on your own, then call a friend and collaborate.

- After it's all been designed, never forget that unless it gleams, people only notice the grime.

- Good housekeeping is saintliness personified.

# 8

# THE WELL-TRAVELLED HOST

"To comprehend one thing and another about his art."

**JOHANN SEBASTIAN BACH**
Explaining his visit to composer Dieterich Buxtehude, 1705.
Bach travelled on foot.

# THE WELL-TRAVELLED HOST

People working in hospitality work very hard, and should take frequent holidays. Busman's holidays.

In a world where everything is always changing, morphing, assimilating, you need the constant provocation and inspiration of new ideas. Take yourself to the elegant Clarence Hotel in Dublin, of a weekend, for instance, and just look at the inspirations that will follow from enjoying the brunch menu concocted by chef Antony Ely. Look at how cleverly these diverse dishes are melded together into an alluring menu, an irresistible menu, indeed. Thinking about it will be almost – almost – as good as eating it.

But inspirations can be found in the most unusual places. Look at the breakfast menu served in the funky Lennon's Café Bar, in Carlow, by Sinéad Byrne and her crew (opposite page). This is a short, sharp masterpiece, a brilliant piece of à la carte breakfast writing, a controlled and enticing offer that could very well fill you with ideas for adapting, changing and improving your own breakfast offer.

So, many fine ideas will lie close to home, and you should always have an eye open for them, ready to bring something back home that can work for you.

But, there is also the wider world to consider searching for new ideas. I don't mean taking a week at Sandy Beach, or chilling out at the Metropolitan or the Four Seasons in New York for a long weekend. Travel, from the French word *travailler*, means to work, and for the person working in hospitality, travel is a method of learning. A busman's holiday.

Johann Sebastian Bach knew there were things he had to learn from his elder composer, Dieterich Buxtehude, so off he went on

# THE WELL-TRAVELLED HOST
## open • your • eyes

**LENNON'S CAFÉ BAR**
**BREAKFAST MENU**

### Cereals

Muesli Special (Natural Yoghurt, plain Muesli, fresh Fruit and Honey); Dried Fruit or plain Muesli with Milk; Porridge with Brown Sugar and Cream

### Open Breakfast Sandwiches (on Toast, Brown or White Soda)

Bacon, Fried Egg, Sausage, Tomato & Clonakilty Black and White Pudding served with tea/coffee

### Croissants, Scones and Toast

Croissant served warm with butter and homemade Jam

Croissant filled with Ham and melted Cheese

Toast or Fruit Scone served with Butter & Jam and Tea or Coffee

### Homemade Cakes and Gateaux

Pear and Almond Tart; Chocolate Brownie; Banoffee; Cookies

### Fresh Juices

Orange, Apple or Cranberry

### Smoothies

Berry, Bio Berry

### Teas/Coffees

Tea (cup); Herbal Tea; Coffee (cup); Coffee (mug); Cappuccino; Double Cappuccino; Latte; Espresso; Double Espresso; Mocha; Viennese; Glass Milk

## THE WELL-TRAVELLED HOST
open • your • eyes

foot to visit the great man. He was gone three months, and got into a whole heap of trouble for the extended absence. But, you might ask, who could teach the almighty Bach anything? Despite his greatness, Bach knew he had to "comprehend one thing and another about his art", his tribute to Buxtehude. No matter how much you know, no matter how much experience you may have, there is always more to know, discover and understand.

Thus, you might take yourself off to the Basque Country or Catalonia in Spain, where the most scintillatingly exciting food is currently being cooked by a dedicated band of brilliant Spanish chefs. Or you might grab a week in Sydney, drawing in ideas like oxygen from the best places to eat, seeing how they do breakfast and brunch, dinner and lunch.

But don't overlook the traditionalists: France and Italy continue to have an enormous amount to offer the curious traveller, simply because the continuation of the culinary and hospitality cultures there is so strong.

Travel will also reveal the ways in which other addresses focus and multiply their offer, how they diversify, and how they create new offers. You might head to Spain, once again, to see how a project such as The Big Stretch, created by experimental psychologist Rosie Walford, and which mixes hiking and walking in the Picos de Europa in Northern Spain with teaching life skills and discussing life issues, may have something to teach you about how to move your hospitality offer in a new, creative and dynamic direction.

So, travel for the busy host is one way to open the mind, but the other aspect of travel that you have to consider is travel in order to get away from the business.

# THE WELL-TRAVELLED HOST
## open • your • eyes

**THE CLARENCE SUNDAY BRUNCH**

Freshly Squeezed Juice: orange, grapefruit, tomato, celery or carrot

Selection of home-made croissants and pastries

Home-made marmalade preserve, and Irish Beeswax honey

•

Baby Gem Salad, Caesar Dressing and Croutons

Creamed Mushrooms on Toasted Mustard Bread

Soft Poached Egg, Toasted Muffin, Hollandaise Sauce

- choice of spinach, smoked salmon, honey roast ham –

Cream of Carrot and Coriander Soup and Garlic Croutons

Fresh Fruit Salad

Selection of Cereals, Hot or Cold Milk

•

Croque Monsieur with Scrambled Egg

Full Irish Breakfast

Salmon and Cod Fishcake, Poached Egg and Seasonal Leaves

Wild Mushroom Risotto with Parmesan and Rocket

Braised Shank of Lamb "Shepherd's Pie"

Grilled Angus Beef Burger and Clarence Chips

•

Mandarin Clafoutis with Crème Fraiche

Chocolate Brownie with Mint Ice Cream

Steamed Sultana Pudding with Crème Anglaise

Vanilla Yoghurt with Apple and Ginger Compote

•

Cocktails: Seabreeze, Cosmopolitan or Bloody Mary

# THE WELL-TRAVELLED HOST
open • your • eyes

## THE WORK-LIFE BALANCE

You also need the holiday holiday, not the busman's holiday. Getting the work-life balance right is one of the most difficult things to achieve in hospitality, a profession that demands long hours and that demands that you are always giving of yourself, and focusing on the demands and needs of other people.

But you, too, have needs and demands, and they must be satisfied, or else you will collapse – in many cases, literally – under the weight of responsibility. So, you must always have an annual holiday, and you must ensure, particularly if you have a young family, that their needs are not sacrificed to the demands of your customers.

When Eugene and Breda MacSweeney ran Kilkenny's Lacken House, for instance, where they had a top-notch destination restaurant along with rooms, they always took a holiday in France at the very height of the season. Lacken would close, the MacSweeneys would pack up the car and the kids, and take off for Europe, and people would say: "Are they nuts? Look at the business they are missing!"

Of course, they were far from nuts; they were right. If you want to give your best in hospitality, and anything less than your best isn't enough, then you have to be fit, relaxed and sharp, and buzzing with new ideas. For every extra day worked through necessity, book yourself an extra day on holiday. You are not a machine, so don't imagine you can behave like one.

Success in hospitality means being in the business for the long haul. Working in hospitality isn't a lifestyle choice, it's a life, so you must have the life and the work in balance, in harmony.

**THE WELL TRAVELLED HOST**
open • your • eyes

# primer

- The busman's holiday is a vital element by which people in hospitality learn what is current, what is new, and what they should know. To learn, you must travel, and experience the work of your contemporaries, both nationally and internationally.

- Travelling doesn't simply mean swanning around 5-star destinations with a glass in your hand. You will often learn the most valuable lessons in the most unlikely places, so keep your eyes open when you are on the road.

- No matter how much you know, no matter how much experience you have, there is always more to know, more to learn, more to understand. Remember J.S. Bach.

- Take rest and recreation breaks often.

- If you do not get the work-life balance right, then hospitality will destroy your health and much else besides. Close the shop!

# TESTIMONY

**Paul Carroll, Ghan House, Carlingford**

## LOVE

• Love what you do. Love that you get to do it. Love your venue, the restaurant, the area, the food, the wine, etc. Take every aspect of the business personally.

• Love to share it with your guests - it is your privilege, not theirs, they are paying to be in your space.

• Eat in your restaurant, sleep in your beds.

## PENGUINS, 30MINS, 350°F

• Think "out of the box." Jump outside yourself, look back at what you have and how you would do it differently if you had the chance. You have the chance. Just do it.

## ORGANIC

• For a long term and stable business, do not be impatient. Let the growth be organic. Live with business decisions, tweak and nurture new directions. If you are good it'll work eventually.

• Invest and think long term.

## CHOICES

• You offer choice on your menu, so think of offering choices on how your customer may use your venue.

• Be creative and open in the way that your space can be used, for example, private dining, tastings, meeting venue, garden barbecue, teambuilding.

## WALKING

• Walking fast should only be done when catching a train. No matter how busy you are, walking fast in the presence of guests does not make you more efficient. Harried and stressed staff create an uncomfortable environment for guests.

## KNOW YOUR INGREDIENTS

• Know your environs and what the area has to offer - history, mythology, restaurants, pubs, drives, walks etc.

• It all adds up to what your business has to offer. Walk the walks, drive the drives, eat in the restaurants. You would not serve a dish not having tasted the ingredients, so actually experience what there is on offer in your area.

## SHARE YOUR LOVE

• Impart your love and vision for your business to your staff.

# TESTIMONY

- This starts at interview stage ensuring you employ like-minded people who look at their work and take care of guests the same way as you do.
This will present a cohesive experience for your guests - likeable, happy staff that are able to share and appreciate with guests the ambience, service, environment, and attitude of the house.

## RELATIONSHIPS

- Create good relationships and know the names of all suppliers, workmen, and delivery personnel. They help provide the infrastructure of the house.

- Treating your meat and vegetable providers, the plumber, the wine supplier, for example, with respect and appreciation is crucial. Make them a cup of tea occasionally. Offer lunch if you are having lunch at the same time.

- All this adds to the reputation you have worked hard to earn and, more importantly, will help with your reputation when you need to get out of a "fix."

## HARD TIMES

- We all make mistakes. Be thankful that a guest told you. Address any issue head on. Listen. Think. Respond.

- If during a busy service time and/or you need time to talk to a member of staff, take details of the complaint, and then deal with it by letter in the cold light of day.

- Handling mistakes quickly with the goodwill of the guest in mind is a tangible measure of your worth and commitment to guest comfort and satisfaction.

## GO, GO GO!

- Try to exceed expectation, don't settle for meeting expectation; Go the extra mile.

- Give personal attention, relate to guests on a personal level. Give them what you would want.

- Be emphatic to guests' needs, whether it be giving them respite or a good time.
Be "in the moment" when chatting to guests.

- Be as welcoming and warming personally as you can be welcoming and warming with your venue – heating, log fires, candlelight, ambient lighting, fluffy towels, crisp linen, great mattresses etc.

- And if you are lucky enough to do all this, for the one you love, never let the one who loves you forget that you love her the most.

# 9

## 9 MARKETING AND MEDIA

> "A critic is a legless man who teaches running."
>
> **CHANNING POLLOCK**

# MARKETING AND MEDIA

In common with many restaurants, the owners of hotels, B&B's and country houses seem to believe that their product will sell itself, as if by magic. Open your doors, and, hey presto! the punters will soon be turning up in their droves, mad keen to enjoy whatever it is that you are doing.

Of course, it doesn't work like that. Nothing works like that. Selling your product needs marketing. You have to get across your message, and not just to the media. You have to market to your existing customers, so that they keep you in mind, and choose you as opposed to some other offer, simply because it has made itself more prominent in their consciousness, or because it is newer. Regular customers are your lifeblood: always bear in mind the maxim of retailing: 80% of your business comes from 20% of your customers.

There is an even more pressing need to try to reach this pinnacle: it costs five times more to secure a new customer than to keep an existing customer. Just as importantly, regular customers are easier to deal with than new customers. They know what you do, they have returned because they like what you do, and consequently they are, even before they walk in the door, relaxed and optimistic: they are looking forward to having a good time.

Newcomers, especially in country houses where there is no space for anonymity, will not be so relaxed, so you have to work much, much harder to introduce them to your *modus operandi*. And, what with having a million things to do each and every day, you can't afford that amount of time with every guest.

To give an example of what I am talking about, here is the sort of customer you want to create.

# MARKETING AND MEDIA
## managing • the • media

### COME HERE OFTEN?

I was once making a bottle for the baby in the utility room of Kelly's Resort Hotel, in Rosslare, during a family holiday. Also in the utility room, packing some laundry into a washing machine, was a sixteen-year-old teenager from Northern Ireland.

We were chatting away when I asked him, as you tend to do in Kelly's, if this was his first visit to the hotel. "Oh no," he said, "this is my sixteenth visit. I've been here every year since I was born."

And he is not alone. Read the Kelly's Resort Hotel Winter Newsletter 2003, for example, and there is a short paragraph about "The Swallows", a group of friends whom, we learn "originally met in the hotel and have been visiting for close to 30 years." So, our teenager from Northern Ireland has some catching up to do.

Now, that sort of customer loyalty is something to die for. So, how do you achieve it?

Well, one of the simplest and cheapest ways in which you achieve it is by staying in touch, by communicating with your customers, by keeping them in the picture about what is new, what is happening, and what has been happening.

The Kelly's Hotel newsletter, for instance, reveals that the hotel has garnered further accolades – best Hotel restaurant for La Marine Bistro; top 20 resort hotels in Britain and Ireland; a prestigious award from America's *Wine Spectator* for their exceptional wine list; it brings us up to date with their new spa development; gives us a simple brown bread recipe; tells us that the dining room has been revamped and renamed Beaches, lets us

## MARKETING AND MEDIA
managing • the • media

know that Kelly's gets through no fewer than 8,000 salmon in a season, and as well as wishing us Merry Christmas, we are subtly given details of their event weekends for the following year.

A newsletter such as this does two things brilliantly: it makes the recipient feel included and respected for their custom, and it provokes them to consider taking a break in Kelly's once again: after all, have you seen the new dining room yet? And you will want to see and try the new spa, won't you? And should you leave the newsletter lying on the kitchen table, you will be certain to hear that familiar refrain: "Mum, when can we go to Kelly's again?"

Just as importantly, the newsletter lets you know that the hotel is not resting on its laurels: improvements, upgrades, developments and awards all spell out one thing: the steady curve of gradual improvement that we have come to expect as the norm in our fevered lives.

## YOUR COMMUNITY

This is the first step towards creating a community amongst your guests, and with the internet, you can do it simply and speedily: a simple newsletter, with straightforward design, can be mailed to hundreds of customers in the blink of an eye.
And what are the rules about getting it right?

Firstly, don't be tempted to do it too often. The internet makes it simple and speedy to send a letter to hundreds of people, but if you send one every month, your customers will quickly get fed up with you. Keep it short and sweet.

# MARKETING AND MEDIA
## managing • the • media

Secondly, don't go in for the hard sell. What you want to convey is simply the impression that you are, and you remain, dynamic, creative, right at the cutting-edge.

For example: a little Christmas card sent electronically by Catherine Fulvio, of Ballyknocken House and cookery school in County Wicklow, one of the best new arrivals in the hospitality world, wishes Mrs Fulvio's customers the compliments of the season, and, at the foot of the card, simply includes details of her recent successes in winning awards and being selected for independent guidebooks. No hard sell, just a note on accolades deservedly won. That's how you do it.

If you pack the letter with offers, discounts, and so on, it will actually work as a turn-off, not a provocation. Remember, you are communicating news to the community of customers, you are not trying to sell them something specific.

Whether you do choose to offer some manner of reward is a personal matter: some element of a discount from the cost of a future package is the sort of thing some places do. Personally, I don't think this is a good idea, as it suggests that your prices could be keener. It is better to keep your value as keen as possible, and remember: you don't want one guest, paying full price, to discover that another guest is there at a discounted rate. That is not the sort of thing that makes people happy.

## MANAGING THE MEDIA

If customers need to be kept up to date with what you are doing, so do the media. But before we consider the position of how to

# MARKETING AND MEDIA
## managing • the • media

develop a relationship with the print and electronic media, let's look at the vital question of how you can get attention for your brand new B&B, country house, hotel or restaurant with rooms.

The normal route taken by many establishments is to hire a firm of public relations consultants. These are the people who are supposedly expert in targeting the correct media, and thereby delivering editorial coverage for your business. They will likely instruct you to have some manner of launch party, or else to address an offer to a specific body of journalists, to come and sample what it is you are doing: in other words, they will suggest that you give this august body of writers something for free.

I don't recommend this approach. First off, it is very expensive, what with the cost of the PR agency's work, followed by the cost of the party or the beano for the journalists. And whilst some PR agencies specialise in the food and tourism sectors and could deliver a good job for you, many agencies won't have that specialist knowledge, and will simply use a scattergun approach, sending info to all and sundry. What all and sundry will do with your expensively printed information is simple: they will remove it from the envelope and put it straight into a bin.

Of course, you could also advertise in the media. But remember the old advertising truth: 50% of the money spent is wasted, but no one knows which 50% is wasted. You can't afford to waste half your money.

There is another way. It works slowly, it works without the hard sell of advertising or public relations, and it works towards achieving editorial coverage, in the media and in guide books. I call it Managing the Media.

Managing the media is based first and foremost on doing your

# MARKETING AND MEDIA
## managing • the • media

job very, very well indeed, so well that what people write about is your skill and success. Myrtle Allen of Ballymaloe House once said to me, "I never did any marketing. I just did my best and hoped that people would like it."

Precisely. Do your best, and you truly have something to market. You are marketing merit, and it is easy to market merit: what is hard to market is a product that doesn't square up.

Think of some of the addresses that seem to endlessly crop up on television, in the newspapers and magazines, in critical reviews, in web newsletters, the places that are the staples of the serious, critical guidebooks. Buggy's Glencairn Inn. The Brook Lodge Inn. Ballyknocken House. Ballymaloe House. The MacNean Bistro. Iskeroon. Ghan House. Kelly's Resort Hotel.

That is simply a handful of places that do something as well as they can, and who manage to get a great deal of coverage for doing it. What they offer varies wildly from place to place, but what they offer is very attractive to the media, and that media, consequently, give these addresses a great deal of valuable – incalculably valuable – coverage.

So, do they all work crazy hard at smooching the media? No, they don't smooch the media at all. What they do is simply to stay in touch with the media, to be pro-active in making sure that the media gets details of whatever new things they are doing, and to stay focused on always making their offer fresh, attractive, something that has a twist, a USP.

Ken Buggy, of Buggy's Glencairn Inn in County Waterford, for example, has demonstrated his irresistible method of making soda bread so often in the media that one could be forgiven for thinking that he is the last man in Ireland making soda bread for

# MARKETING AND MEDIA
## managing • the • media

his guests. Of course he isn't, but his wit, originality and geniality make him a must-have on every television director's shortlist of targets. And every time the camera is on him, or the journalist is sitting there primed for a pithy quote, Mr Buggy, despite his inherent shyness, delivers a performance. And that is what managing the media is about: a performance.

If the media know of you, know that you have a USP, an attitude, an opinion, then they will beat a regular path to your door and you will profit handsomely from their attention.

Of course, there will be times when you are under pressure when they call, and you would ideally like them to go away. It is at exactly that moment that you must turn on the performance, just as you would turn on a tap. You step outside yourself, into the performer whose job it is to convey your message. Not the person doing the hard sell, but the person whose expertise, skill and experience makes their opinion valuable. Remember, it's not about selling: it's about communicating.

You do it like this: buy all the newspapers, and all the magazines that deal with food, travel and hospitality, trawl through them, surf the net, and select individual targets that might have an interest in knowing who you are, where you are, and what you do. Do the same with the electronic media: travel programmes, current affairs programmes, specialist media.

Travel editors, especially those who write short pieces of travel and holiday info, are especially valuable people to communicate with. But individual travel, food and hospitality writers throughout the media can be especially glad of being presented with an interesting story.

# MARKETING AND MEDIA
## managing • the • media

And don't expect to get coverage immediately: they may well file your info away to return to it at some future date. So, don't give up just because George in *The Daily Telegraph* or Arthur in *The New York Times Magazine* hasn't responded to your mail or letter: St Patrick's Day will come around next year, and you could well be just the sort of person and place that George or Arthur needs to fill his editorial right then.

Quality guide books, where the editors pay their way, are potentially the most important method of spreading news of your existence that you can get. So, write to them, let them know the who, where and when, and always keep them up to date with any changes. Guidebook writers love addresses that communicate consistently and succinctly. And, once you are described in one quality guide book, the others inevitably follow suit.

No PR company needed, no advertising budget to make the bank manager nervous. It is simply simple communication, founded on the confidence that you are doing something right, something that people will like, and that writers will like to write about.

So, direct communication with specific individuals in media zones that have an interest in conveying your information is how you take media management forward. And you not only do it slowly, you do it consistently.

## WORKING TOGETHER

There is another method of media management that has proven efficacy. It happens when a group of people in the hospitality

## MARKETING AND MEDIA
**managing • the • media**

and restaurant business work together to promote their individual town or region.

The instigator of this approach in Ireland was the Kinsale Good Food Circle, a powerful grouping of creative restaurateurs who were fundamental in creating the culinary reputation of Kinsale, and of maintaining its position as a destination address, something they achieved for a couple of decades. Even today, when the culinary reputation of the town has been overtaken by other places, Kinsale is still associated in many visitors' minds with creative cooking, and is thereby a destination of choice.

More recently, a bunch of restaurateurs and hospitality operators have had considerable success in promoting West Waterford as a destination zone. This project began with an energetic local LEADER group, who brought together a coalition of addresses known as The West Waterford Good Food Tree.

They published a critical guide to their individual addresses and promoted it, with the result that within a few years this region, which previously had no reputation as a destination address, either for tourism or especially for good food, had become successfully identified in the public eye with creative, imaginative cookery and great hospitality.

And not only does such an identification attract tourists, it also attracts other tourism operators, who see the region as being virgin territory with lots of potential. Other smart restaurateurs and hospitality operators have opened in West Waterford in recent years, attracted not just by its beauty, but also by its potential, and by the openness of the other operators there, who were first to realise the benefits of collaboration. This is how

## MARKETING AND MEDIA
### managing • the • media

you build critical mass, the series and variety of addresses within a given region that increases the attraction of the region to the traveller.

What they did in West Waterford was based on quality: each member had to be of a comparable standard to each other member, whether they ran a country house, a restaurant or a pub. This is a vital characteristic of any successful grouping, because it means that the B&B keeper can genuinely recommend the restaurant nearby that is also a member of the group.

This is a key element of the deal: what you are trying to achieve is to, firstly, attract people to the region and, secondly, you want to keep them there for as long as possible. This requires the ability to give them a range of choices, all of which have to be good. If you are recommending the local restaurant simply because it is run by your sister-in-law, and if your guests go there and have a bad experience, they blame both the restaurant, and you, for making the recommendation. Do this, and you both lose out, and the visitor won't be back: it's strictly lose-lose.

But, if you can trust the quality of the restaurant, and if the guests have a good dinner and are in a good mood the next morning and are grateful to you, they suddenly have a whole different picture of what is on offer. Now, it's not just win-win, for you and the restaurant, it's win-win-win-win: B&B, restaurant, customer, region.

Collaboration within a LEADER grouping is a good place to start such a group, but the critical thing that adjacent tourism operators must appreciate is that they are not in competition with one another. West Waterford restaurateurs and B&B

**MARKETING AND MEDIA**
managing • the • media

keepers are not in competition with each other: they are in competition with Kinsale and Killarney, Clifden and the Tipperary lakelands, and, on a broader scale, they are in competition with cheap flights to and weekend breaks in Paris and Brussels, or package deals in Tuscany or the Lake District.

# primer

- **Every address in hospitality needs to market itself, both to customers and to the media.**

- **It costs five times as much to bag a new customer as it does to keep an existing customer, so look after the regulars first.**

- **A newsletter creates a community amongst your customers and makes them feel special.**

- **If you feel the need to hire public relations consultants to promote your business, make sure to hire a firm that specialises in food, travel and tourism. Otherwise, you will simply be wasting your money.**

- **Bringing media management in house is effective:**

## MARKETING AND MEDIA
managing • the • media

But, if they work together to promote their zone, they have a greater chance of succeeding, and of promoting their attractions to a global audience. I mean, the smart trip these days is a direct flight into Waterford and a weekend eating, staying and exploring this glorious place. Paris? So passé, dear.

**cost-effective; response-effective; time-effective. It's also more fun.**

**• With the media, you have to tell them, tell them again, then tell them that you have told them. Repetition is boring, but effective.**

**• Having a quirky USP makes media management simple, but don't be gimmicky: gimmicks soon run out of steam.**

**• Work within your community of hospitality providers to market your area as a destination. You want people to come to your zone, and to stay there for as long as possible. That way, everyone prospers.**

**• You are not in competition with other hospitality providers in your area: your competition in tourism is the whole wide world.**

# APPENDIX AND RECIPES

"He ordered as one to the menu born."

O HENRY

# APPENDIX

# Don't forget...

- The first contact with the customer is the most important moment of the entire hospitality relationship. The first response to an enquiry via e-mail, the first greeting when you answer the telephone, the first welcome as guests arrive in the door, are all pivotal moments. Get it right, and life is easy. Get it wrong, and you will be struggling with the guests for the entire duration of their stay.

- Front-line staff at reservations and reception are the heart of the operation. They have first contact with the guests, and last contact with the guests, so what the guests are saying as they swing out of the driveway depends on how the front desk handled the farewells, and the greeting.

- Never talk over the heads of children, by addressing a question to their parents. Offer children menus first, and make sure the kids are happy, for happy kids equals happy parents. Oh, and the kids are your future customers.

- In really good hotels, the customer is the second most important person. For the owner, the staff must always be the most important consideration. If the staff are happy, they over-deliver, and then the customer is happy. If the staff are not happy, they under-deliver, and the whole thing falls flat. Staff first, customers second.

    Really expert people never let on to the customer that they

# APPENDIX
don't forget

are anything other than the most important person in the world.

• A complaint is a blessing. It sure doesn't seem like it at the time, but the complaint is a forewarning of a problem that can be fixed. So, always thank the customer for drawing your attention to the problem. You might even suggest that they might like to switch careers, and get a real job in hospitality.

• Flat-line management is the only way to succeed: nobody is too important to carry bags or to help out behind the bar or to light the fire. Hierarchies are inimical to good hospitality.

• If you have fires, light them.
A fire is not just a source of heat, it is also a source of psychological welcome and comfort. In the best addresses, the fires are lit continuously. A fire that is doing nothing is depressing, and makes the owners seem mean.

• In hospitality, everyone is part of the crew, and communication within the crew is vital to success: keep everyone posted, keep everyone up to speed.

• Exceed expectations: aim for the Wow! Factor.

• WOM (Word of Mouth) is the most powerful marketing tool known to man. And it's free.

• If you aren't retaining your customers, something is not working properly. "Nice to have you back" is the happiest phrase in hospitality.

# APPENDIX

Here are some practical and useful breakfast and brunch recipes that we have collected over the last 15 years or so, writing about chefs and hospitality in Ireland.

## CRÈME FRAÎCHE

**This is Bernadette O'Shea's recipe for Crème Fraîche from her book *Pizza Defined*.**

3 parts fresh cream to 1 part buttermilk

Both at room temperature

**METHOD:** Combine the cream and buttermilk and cover with cling film.
- Leave at room temperature for 12 hours
- Remove thickened crème fraîche to glass jug with tight-fitting lid and refrigerate.
- It will hold for about 6 days.

## GER FOOTE'S CLARIFIED BUTTER

**This process removes the milk solids from butter and means it will not burn at higher temperatures, such as those needed to properly baste eggs.**

**METHOD:** Cut butter into cubes, then melt slowly in a saucepan. White solids will float to the top. Strain the butter through the finest mesh sieve you have.
- One pound of butter will yield about 1½ cups of clarified butter.

## DILISK BREAD

**We created this recipe for the first Irish Food Guide in 1989.**

350 g (12 oz) wholemeal flour

50 g (2 oz) white flour

25 g (1 oz) oatmeal

1 teaspoon salt

1 teaspoon bicarbonate of soda

small handful of washed, finely chopped dilisk

300-450 ml (½ to ¾ pint) buttermilk

**METHOD:** Place the flours and oatmeal in a bowl, with the salt and soda.
- Stir in the dilisk and pour in the buttermilk.
- Bring the mixture together until it forms a moist ball of dough, but don't knead.
- Place on a greased baking tray, cut a cross through the top, making a deep indentation, and bake in a hot oven, 200°C/425°F/mark 7, for about 35-40 minutes, until the bread sounds hollow when you tap it.

# APPENDIX

### EMILY GREEN'S EGGS BENEDICT

Eggs Benedict is a classic, but rarely seen now, though a superb version of it is still offered in Newport House, in Newport, County Mayo. It is richness and indulgence personified. American writer, Emily Green, who is the food writer for the *LA Times*, writes that "The recipe has always been used for my family's Easter lunch. My mother reserved the egg whites left over from the sauce making and made meringues for dessert, served with fruit salad. To accompany the eggs Benedict we would have the first new season asparagus. I now serve the same every year, which is about as often as it is advisable to eat such a rich meal."

*Ingredients to serve 4*

salt

juice of 1 small lemon, or to taste

12 medium-sized fresh eggs

250 g (9 oz) butter

finely ground white pepper to taste

8 rashers of smoked bacon

4 muffins or 8 crumpets

¼ teaspoon malt or wine vinegar

finely chopped parsley

**METHOD:** To make the hollandaise sauce, dissolve a good pinch or two of salt in lemon juice.
- Separate four eggs, reserving only the yolks (you can use the whites for the meringues).
- Melt butter in a small saucepan.
- Place yolks in the bowl of the food processor.
- Pulse the motor once or twice to blend, then run the blender on low as you add the lemon juice and white pepper, followed by the butter in a slow stream, as if making mayonnaise.
- Stop blending as the mixture thickens into a rich emulsion.
- Adjust seasoning and reserve the sauce in a warm spot.
(If the sauce curdles, which it should not but might do, stir in a small lump of ice.)
- Grill bacon.
- Split and toast muffins.
- Put one slice of bacon atop each muffin half and reserve on plates in a warm oven.
- Fill a large shallow frying pan with boiling water from the kettle. Keep on the verge of boiling over a low to medium flame.
- Holding each egg in a slotted spoon, dip in the boiling water for 30 seconds, then

# APPENDIX

return to counter to cool before cracking.
- When each egg has been primed for poaching, top up water if necessary and add 1 teaspoon vinegar (this is an important acid for cooking the very alkaline eggs, and will not taste much in the final dish).
- Cook two eggs at a time. Attempting more is a recipe for a mess. Crack eggs and gently slide each on to a saucer.
- From the saucer, slide it gently into the simmering water. Turning the eggs will cook the white more evenly over the yolk.
- Once the albumen is silky and white, remove the egg with a slotted spoon.
- Drain the eggs, trim any particularly straggly bits and place them in the oven atop the waiting muffin and bacon.
- Continue the poaching operation until each muffin is topped.
- Spoon over the hollandaise and top with finely chopped parsley.

## HERB QUIGLEY'S AMERICAN/IRISH BREADS

These are some of the most imaginative and interesting bread recipes we know, given to us by Herb and Christine Quigley, who for some years ran Ballycormac House in County Tipperary, which was known for its special bread courses.

Herb used Ballybrado's rye and wheat flour and Doves Farm strong white flour for all his breads. "Both mills produce consistently exceptional flours," he says.

## SPICED RYE BREAD

**Herb and Chris used this bread to accompany smoked salmon and rhubarb mousse.**

5 teaspoons active dry yeast

1 3/4 cup of warm water

2 teaspoons salt

1/2 teaspoon ground cloves

1/2 teaspoon ground allspice

1/4 teaspoon ground cinnamon

1 teaspoon caraway seeds

2 tablespoons brown sugar

3 tablespoons molasses

2 tablespoons shortening

2 1/2 cups rye flour

3-3 1/2 cups strong white flour

# APPENDIX

**METHOD:** Prove yeast in warm water for ten minutes until foamy.
- In a large bowl combine salt, cloves, allspice, cinnamon, caraway, sugar and molasses.
- Blend in shortening, add yeast mixture, rye flour and 1 cup white flour.
- Beat with a wooden spoon until smooth.
- Continue to add white flour until dough cleans the sides of the bowl and is sticky but firm.
- Knead for eight minutes on a lightly floured surface.
- Place in a greased bowl, cover with cling wrap and let rise until doubled, about 1 hour.
- Divide the dough into two parts and roll each into an oblong shape and place on greased baking sheet.
- Cover with a tea towel and let rise until doubled, about 45 minutes.
- With a sharp knife or razor slash the top of the loaves into a pattern.
- Bake at 190°C/375°F/mark 5 for 45 minutes, until the bottom of the loaf sounds hollow when tapped.
- Remove from sheets to racks to cool.

### SEMOLINA BREAD
**This bread keeps well and makes very nice toast.**

2½ teaspoons active dry yeast

¼ cup warm water

1 tablespoon olive oil

1 teaspoon malt syrup

1 cup water

2½ cups semolina

1 cup strong white flour

2 teaspoons salt

⅓ cup sesame seeds

**METHOD:** Dissolve yeast in warm water and prove for 10 minutes until foamy.
- In a large bowl combine the yeast mixture, oil, malt, and 1 cup water.
- In another bowl sift together the semolina, flour and salt.
- Mix 1 cup of the flour mixture at a time into the liquid.
- Beat with a wooden spoon until smooth.
- Knead 8-10 minutes, occasionally slamming the dough down to develop the gluten.

# APPENDIX

- Place dough in a lightly oiled bowl, covered with cling wrap, and let rise until doubled, about 1½ hours.
- The dough will be springy and blistered but still soft.
- Punch down the dough, knead one minute, and let it rest five minutes.
- Flatten into a square and roll into a long narrow rope - about 20 inches long. (The dough will be very elastic). Cut rope in half and shape into two loaves by rolling each rope into a 1½ inch diameter rope.
- Coil into a figure that looks like an inverted "S".
- Place the loaves on oiled baking sheets.
- Brush the surface lightly with water and sprinkle with sesame seeds; press seeds gently into dough.
- Cover with a tea towel and let rise until doubled, about one hour.
- Preheat the oven to 220°C/425°F/mark 7.
- Place baking sheet in oven and throw three ice cubes into the bottom of the oven - then immediately close the door.
- Bake for ten minutes.
- Reduce the heat to 200°C/400°F/mark 6 and bake for 25-30 minutes, until the loaves sound hollow when tapped.
- Cool on racks.

### JANE JACKMAN'S FRENCH TOAST

3 eggs

¼ pint of milk

vanilla extract

cinnamon

½ loaf challah (egg enriched white bread) broken into pieces

butter

icing sugar

**METHOD:** Beat the eggs. Add the milk and mix together.
- Flavour the egg/milk mixture with a drop of vanilla extract and a pinch of cinnamon.
- Leave the torn-up pieces of challah to soak in the mixture.
- Melt a large knob of butter in a non-stick frying pan and fry the pieces of bread until they are crisp, remove and dust with icing sugar.

# APPENDIX

### LUCY MADDEN'S CINNAMON POTATO BUNS
"A cross between an Eccles cake and a croissant" is how Lucy describes these buns.

225 g (8 oz) potatoes, cooked and puréed
110 g (4 oz) butter
90 g (3½ oz) sugar
275 ml (½ pint) milk
2 teaspoons salt
2 eggs
1.125 kg (2 ½ lb) flour
1 packet quick-action yeast

*Filling Ingredients:*
110 g (4 oz) granulated sugar
1 teaspoon cinnamon
100 g (4 oz) raisins
110 g (4 oz) light brown sugar
110 g (4 oz) chopped walnuts
100 g (4 oz) butter, melted

**METHOD:** Place the potatoes, butter, sugar, salt and milk in the bowl of a food processor and mix well.
- Add the beaten eggs, the flour and the yeast and enough tepid water to make a pliable dough.
- Place in an airtight container in a warm place overnight.
- Divide the dough into two parts. Roll each part out into a thin rectangle about quarter of an inch thick.
- Mix the sugar and cinnamon and sprinkle over the dough.
- Add the raisins, brown sugar and nuts.
- Drizzle the butter over the whole surface and roll up as for a roulade.
- Cut into half inch slices and place side by side in a well-greased pan.
- Allow to rise again.
- Bake at gas 190°C/375°F/mark 5 for 20-25 minutes. Irresistible!

# APPENDIX

### ELEPHANT AND CASTLE EGGS IPANEMA, WITH AVOCADO AND FRIED BANANA

**This recipe was given to us by Liz Mee, the original owner of the Elephant and Castle in Dublin.**

*Ingredients to serve 2*

225 g (8 oz) fillet steak, grilled, then sliced and arranged in overlapping slices

1 avocado, sliced thinly and fanned on two plates

2 small bananas cooked in butter until golden brown

4 eggs, fried sunny-side up

hollandaise sauce (see page 172)

chives, snipped

2 slices of orange

**METHOD:** Place the sliced fillet on the plates alongside the avocado. Add the fried banana and the fried eggs.
- Garnish with 1 tablespoon of hollandaise on each plate over the avocado, then sprinkle with chives.
- Finally, add a twist of orange to each plate.

The following five recipes are for brunch, and were given to us by Ben Gorman of The Mermaid Café in Dublin.

### THE MERMAID ANGELS ON HORSEBACK

This is Ben's recipe for this classic dish.
- Open as many oysters as you wish or can afford.
- Reserve the liquor as it is precious and delicious.
- Wrap each oyster in streaky smoked bacon and secure it with a satay or cocktail stick.
- Grill it lightly until the bacon is cooked.
- Roll in some toasted breadcrumbs and serve.

# APPENDIX

**JOHNNY CAKES WITH WHITE PUDDING, QUAIL'S EGGS AND SPINACH**

**The Johnny Cakes are a slightly lighter, modernised version of an old classic new England recipe.**

*Ingredients for the Johnny Cakes (makes about 12 small cakes):*

4 eggs

70g (2½ oz) yellow corn meal

30g (1¼ oz) white cornmeal or strong white flour

400ml (14 fl oz) cold milk

dash brandy

chopped fresh dill

salt and pepper

corn oil

*For each Johnny cake:*

garlic, finely chopped

knob of butter

55g (2oz) spinach

salt & pepper

2 slices White pudding

1 quail's egg

**METHOD:** Beat the eggs in a bowl with the corn meal and flour.
- When it is a smooth paste, add the cold milk, the brandy and the herbs and seasonings.
- Cook the cakes in small galette pans with corn oil to make them similar to thick baby pancakes. Leave to cool.

*Assembling the dish:*
- Sauté some chopped garlic in butter, add the spinach, season and toss until cooked.
- Slice the white pudding and fry it gently in a pan.
- Arrange the spinach on each cake, leaving a well in the centre for the quail's egg.
- Break an egg carefully into the well and put two pieces of white pudding to each side. Place under the grill until the egg is just cooked.

# APPENDIX

### QUICK SOURDOUGH PANCAKES
### WITH CINNAMON AND HONEY ORANGE SALAD

Ben Gorman cooks real sourdough pancakes in The Mermaid, but to do that you will need a sourdough starter, which can take weeks to achieve. So instead Ben offers this "quick" sourdough recipe in which yoghurt and baking soda give a similar sour note and lightness to the pancakes. It's a terrific pancake recipe, and makes splendid kid's food also. A tactile brunch.

4 whole eggs
100 g (4 oz) plain flour
1 level teaspoon baking soda (sifted)
300 ml ($^1/_2$ pint) milk
100 ml ($3^1/_2$ fl oz) low fat yoghurt
pinch of salt
pinch of sugar
dash of brandy

**METHOD:** Whisk together the eggs, then beat in flour, with baking soda.
• As you whisk add milk and yoghurt. Season with a pinch of salt, sugar and a dash of brandy.
• Cover, set aside and allow the mixture to rest.
• You can cook this batter as thick or as thin as you like, advises Ben. "I have tried everything from my biggest frying pans to my smallest blini pans but I now stick to my small skillets. They end up about 6" in diameter and are thicker than crepes and a little thinner than blinis".
• To cook the pancakes, rub a well-seasoned pan with vegetable oil using kitchen paper, and cook over a medium heat until perforations appear in the surface, then flip over and cook the other side.
• They should be gently tanned by the heat.
• Keep warm in a low oven as you make the remaining pancakes.
• The first one you make will, of course, always stick to the pan and have to be chucked out.

# APPENDIX

### HOT CINNAMON AND HONEY ORANGE SALAD

750 mls (1 ¼ pints) orange juice
250 g (9 oz) honey (orange flower honey, for purists)
1 stick cinnamon
2 star anise pods
6 oranges

**METHOD:** In a stainless steel pan, reduce the orange juice with the honey, cinnamon and star anise pods to approximately half its original quantity. This becomes your "dressing".
• To make the salad, simply peel the oranges with a knife so as to remove all the pith, and cut them into wagon wheel shapes.
• Warm them gently in the rich orange sauce and pour over the pancakes.
• Serve them with a good dollop of Greek yogurt or crème fraiche.
• Mr Gorman adds: "Avoid the temptation of adding Cointreau. This is brunch, not after-dinner crêpes suzette!"

# APPENDIX

### DISH SMOKED CHICKEN HASH, BASTED EGGS, HOLLANDAISE, SLICED MELON

Here is a perfect example of what brunch is all about. With no other meal would you even think of mixing these ingredients - melon, smoked chicken, hollandaise, basted eggs - but the mixture of savoury and sweet is the secret of brunch, and of this knock-out combination from Dublin restaurant Dish, and its chef, Ger Foote.

### INGREDIENTS FOR THE CHICKEN HASH

500 g (1 lb) smoked chicken breast, shredded with a fork
1 Spanish onion, finely chopped
3 red peppers, finely chopped
3 tablespoons clarified butter
$1/8$ cup plain flour
$1/3$ cup dry white wine
$1 1/2$ cups cream
$1/2$ teaspoon cayenne pepper
fine sea salt to taste
$1/4$ cup finely chopped flat leaf parsley, (leaves only)

### THE HOLLANDAISE

3 sprigs flat leaf parsley
3 small shallots, finely chopped
$1/2$ cup dry white wine
$1/2$ cup white wine vinegar
3 egg yolks
1 cup clarified butter
1 tablespoon lemon juice
salt and white pepper

# APPENDIX

## BASTED EGGS

1 cup olive oil

1 cup clarified butter

eggs (number depending on how many are eating)

**METHOD:** To make the hollandaise sauce, combine parsley sprigs, shallots, white wine and vinegar in a pan and bring to the boil over high heat and reduce to 2 tablespoons of liquid. Remove from heat and strain. Reserve liquid.

- Whisk eggs yolks until very light coloured and trebled in volume.
- Slowly add clarified butter whisking all the time. When three quarters of the butter has been added, thin out with lemon juice. Continue with butter and finally add wine vinegar reduction. Season with salt and white pepper.

*For Smoked Chicken Hash*

- Cook the onion and pepper in the clarified butter in a large sauté pan with a cover, over medium heat, until softened and the onion has become translucent.
- Sprinkle the flour over and cook, stirring, for 4-5 minutes.
- Add shredded smoked chicken breast and cook for 1 more minute.
- Gradually add wine stirring all the time and cook until the mixture becomes quite thick.
- Add cream and cook over medium heat until thickened.
- Season with the cayenne pepper, salt to taste, and stir in finely chopped flat leaf parsley.
- To cook the eggs, gently heat oil and butter together, the amount needed depending on how many eggs you are cooking. When quite hot (but not frying temperature) break eggs into pan and slowly cook, basting all the time. When just soft, remove and serve hot.

*To Serve*

- Serve the smoked chicken hash with the basted eggs, wedges of honeydew melon and hollandaise sauce.

# BIBLIOGRAPHY

**Allen, Darina.** *Irish Traditional Food.* Gill & Macmillan, Dublin 1995; *Ballymaloe Cookery Course.* Gill & Macmillan, Dublin, 2001

**Ayto, John.** *The Glutton's Glossary.* Routledge, London, 1990

**Carluccio, Antonio.** *A Passion for Mushrooms.* Pavilion/Michael Joseph, London 1989

**Cedroni, Moreno.** *Sushi & Suchi.* Bibliotheca Culinaria, Lodi, 2003

**Connery, Clare.** *In an Irish Country Kitchen.* Weidenfeld & Nicholson, London, 1992

**Cowan, Cathal & Sexton, Regina.** *Ireland's Traditional Foods.* Teagasc, Dublin 1997

**David, Elizabeth.** *An Omelette and a Glass of Wine.* Penguin, London, 1986

**De Pomiane, Edouard.** *Cooking in Ten Minutes.* Lilliput Press, Dublin 1993

**Dupleix, Jill.** *Favourite Food.* Conran Octopus, London, 1998

**Flynn, Paul.** *An Irish Adventure with Food.* Collins Press, Cork, 2003

**Granger, Bill.** *Sydney Food; Bill's Food; Bill's Open Kitchen.*

Murdoch Books, Sydney, 2001-2003

**Harris, Henry.** *The Fifth Floor Cookbook.* 4th Estate, London, 1998

**Irwin, Florence.** *The Cookin' Woman.* Blackstaff Press, Belfast, 1986

**Madison, Deborah.** *Vegetarian Cooking for Everyone.*

Broadway Books, New York, 1997

**McKenna, Sally & McKenna, John.** *The Irish Food Guide.* Anna Livia Press, Dublin, 1989; *The Bridgestone 100 Best Places to Stay in Ireland,* 1992-2004; *The Bridgestone Irish Food Guide* 1991, 1993, 1996, 1999; *The Bridgestone Food Lovers Guides to Ireland.* Estragon Press, Durrus, 1991-2004

# BIBLIOGRAPHY

**Mennell, Stephen.** *All Manners of Food.* Illini Books, Illinois, 1996

**Olney, Richard.** *Simple French Food.* Grub Street, London 2003

   *The Good Cook: Techniques and Recipes.* Time-Life Books, Alexandria, Va. 1979

**O'Shea, Bernadette.** *Pizza Defined.* Estragon Press, Durrus, 1997

**Pirie, Gayle and Clark, John.** *Country Egg, City Egg.* Artisan, New York, 2000

**Visser, Margaret.** *The Rituals of Dinner.* Grove Weidenfeld, New York, 1991

**Ypma, Herbert.** *Hip Hotels, City.* Thames & Hudson, London, 1999.

# INDEX

AA Roadwatch  90
Access  19
Adare  22
Adria, Ferran  136
Aida  91
Aleph  20
Allen, Darina  51, 62
Allen, Myrtle  99
Amansara  136
An Omelette and a Glass of Wine  127
Annascaul Black Pudding  54
Anonymous 4  91
Apple Farm, The  80
Ash Rowan  56, 57
Assolas Country House  81, 137
Aughrim  116
Austin, Karen  82

Bach, Johann Sebastian  91, 143, 144, 146
Bagenalstown  87
Ballyconneely  74
Ballycormac House  62, 75
Ballyknocken House & Cookery School  92, 157, 159
Ballymaloe Cookery School  41, 51, 80
Ballymaloe House  37, 41, 99, 159
Ballymote  100
Ballynahinch Castle  40, 101, 104
Bandon  74

Bannocks  66
Banyan Tree, The  136
Barbados  136
Barnes, Sally  76
Barry's of Cork  56
Bartels, Adriaan  125
Basque Country  146
Baylough  89
Beaches Restaurant  139
Bed and Breakfast  50
Bedford, Sybille  71
Beeton, Isabella  102
Belfast  91
Belvelly Smokehouse  74
Bierce, Ambrose  12, 13
Bievres  114
Big Stretch, The  146
Bill Casey's Smoked Fish  74
Bill's Food  72
Bill's Open Kitchen  15, 72
Bircher Muesli  84
Blake, Beatrice  139
Blindgate House  33, 139
Bloom, Leopold  79
Boilie  89
Borges, Jorge Luis  20
Bourke, Hazel  81
Boxty  64
Breakfast  54

# INDEX

*Bridgestone 100 Best Places to Stay in Ireland* **27, 98**
*Bridgestone Guides* **36, 51**
Brook Lodge Inn, The **33, 112, 159**
Brown Thomas **37**
Bruckless **30**
Brulé, Tyler **38**
Brussels **164**
Buggy, Cathleen **52**
Buggy, Ken **59, 77**
Buggy, Ken and Cathleen **33**
Buggy's Glencairn Inn **52, 59, 159**
Buxtehude, Dieterich **143, 144, 146**
Byrne, Sinéad **144**

**Caherbeg Free Range Pork 54**
Calman, Mel **37**
Carlingford **41, 150**
Carlow, County **36, 135, 144**
Carluccio, Antonio **73**
*Carmen* **91**
Carroll, Paul **41, 150**
Casey, Bill, Smoked Fish **74**
Castle Leslie **37, 62**
Castlemurray House **30**
Castletownshend **74**
Catalonia **146**
Cedroni, Moreno **73**
Cesare, Pio **72**

Charleville **53**
Clare, County **74**
Clarence Hotel, The **40, 137, 144, 147**
Clarke's of Ballina **74**
Classic Breakfast Breads **66**
Classic FM **90**
Clifden **138**
CNN **39**
Coakley, Maeve **139**
Coast Townhouse **33, 137**
Cobh **74**
Compote, The **81**
*Concise Oxford Dictionary* **111**
Connell, Violet **33**
Connemara **40, 101, 104, 137**
Connemara Smokehouse **74**
Continuous Improvement **120**
Conway, Shelagh **140**
Coolea **89**
Cowan, Cathal **60**
Creedon, Donal **86**
Customise **21**

***Daily Telegraph, The* 161**
Davenport, Philippa **85**
Davern, Donagh **120, 132**
David, Elizabeth **73, 127, 128**
de Pomiane, Edouard **89**
Delcros, Thierry and Claire **31**

# INDEX

Delphi Lodge  40
Destination  36
Dingle Peninsula  39
Dlugacz's Butcher's Shop  79
Dolphin Beach  138
Donegal, County  31
Donnybrook Church  112
Dougan, Jilly  55
Doyle, Bernard  112
Doyle, Eoin  112
Doyle, Evan  33, 112
Drambuie  86
Dublin  136, 137, 140, 144
Dungarvan  54, 83
Dunn's of Dublin  74
Durrus Cheese  89

**Earl Grey Tea**  74
Echo Lodge  33
Egg  69
Ely, Antony  144
Emin, Tracey  111
Ennis  120
Equinox  91
Eriksson, Caroline  38

**Fadge**  67
Fagan, Declan and Bernadette  40
Farmers' Market  113

Feel-Good Factor  119
Feng Shui  136
Fermoyle Lodge  137
Finnan Haddie  77
Fish  74
Flynn, Paul  73
Fortview House  33, 65
Four Seasons, The  144
Foyle, Paddy and Julia  33
France  146
Friedman, Vanessa  19
Fruit  80
Full Irish, The  90
Fulvio, Catherine  92, 157

**Geoghegan, Joe**  76
Germany  138
Ghan House  41, 150, 159
Glencairn Inn  77
Goleen  33, 65
Good Things Café  61
Grains  84
Granger, Bill  15, 71, 84, 89
Grenadine  82
Gubbeen Smokehouse  54
Gubbeen Cheese  89
Guggi  139

**Hacienda Benazazu**  136

# INDEX

Haddock, Smoked  76
Hanora's Cottage  **40, 79**
Hazlet, Sam and Evelyn  57
Hederman, Frank 76
Hempel, The  136
Henry, O  167
Herbert, A. P.  49
Hewitt, Angela  91
Hilton, Conrad  **32, 46**
Hobbs, Keith  33
Hofstader, Richard  **17, 18**
Horseleap  40
Hotel de Crillon  19
Howley, Marguerite  31

**Identity  36**
Information  19
*Irish Food Guide, The*  27
Irish Mist  86
Irish Slow Food Presidia  74
Irish Smoked Wild Atlantic Salmon  74
Iskeroon  **39, 138, 159**
ISWAS (Irish Smoked Wild Atlantic Salmon)  74
Italy  146

**Japanese Breakfast  88**
Java Republic  56
John David Power's Smoked Bacon  54

Johnson, Samuel  25
Journalists  158
Joyce, James  79

**Kanturk  81**
Kelly, Bill  46
Kelly's Resort Hotel  **40, 46, 139, 155, 159**
Kenmare  **125, 137**
Kennan, Frank and Rosemary  100
Kerry, County  **125, 137**
Kilgraney Country House  **36, 87, 135**
Kilkenny  **75, 115, 119, 148**
Killarney  **115, 119**
Killarney Park Hotel, The  **112, 119, 137**
Kinsale  **33, 139**
Kinsale Good Food Circle  162
Kinvara Organic Smoked Salmon  74
Kunze, Otto and Hilda  40

**La Marine Bistro  155**
La Mere Poulard  **70, 71**
Lacken House  **75, 148**
Lake District  164
Laois, County  100
Las Vegas  101
LEADER  162
Leader, Daniel  58
Leech, Bryan  36

# INDEX

Lennon's Café Bar  **144, 145**
Leslie, Sammy  **37**
Lettercollum House  **82**
Letterfrack  **40**
Lewis, Rosa  **107**
Lichtenberg, G. C.  **11**
Limerick  **135**
*Linoleum\*™*  **20**
Lisdoonvarna Smokehouse  **74**
Loughrea  **90**
Lynch, Gearoid  **33**

**MacNean Bistro, The**  **159**
Macreddin Village  **112**
Macroom Oatmeal  **86**
MacSweeney, Eugene and
 Breda  **75, 148**
Madame Poulard  **70, 71**
Maguire, Neven  **32**
Managing the Media  **158**
Marble Hall  **140**
Marketing  **154**
Marley, Martin  **36**
Mayo  **137**
Mayo, County  **74**
McKenna, PJ  **26**
McLoughlin, Con  **82**
McMeel, Noel  **62**
Meadowsweet Organic Eggs  **55**

Media  **154**
Mennell, Stephen  **132**
Metropolitan, The  **144**
Miami  **136**
Miso Soup  **88**
Monaghan  **62**
Mont St Michel  **70**
*Morning Ireland*  **90**
Morrison, The  **33, 40, 137**
Moyallon Foods  **55**
Mozart  **91**
Muesli  **84**
Mullane, Dan  **22, 33**
Murray's of Charleville  **53**
Mustard Seed, The  **22, 137**

**Nadelson, Reggie**  **53**
New York  **136, 144**
*New York Times*  **97**
*New York Times Magazine, The*  **161**
Newport House  **40, 137**
Nire Valley  **40**
Nordic Breakfast  **88**
North Cork  **53, 86, 137**
Northern Ireland  **86**
*Nota Bene*  **20, 136**

**O'Doherty, Pat**  **54**
O'Flaherty, Patrick  **104**

# INDEX

Offal  79
Old Ground, The  120
Olde Post Inn, The  32
Olney, Richard  **69, 70**
Ong, Christina  134
Orchard Café  119
Otto's Creative Catering  40

**Parapluies in Cocktails  38**
Paris  **114, 164**
Pat O'Doherty's Black Bacon  54
*Pearl Fishers, The*  91
Perahia, Murray  91
Perceval, Sandy and Deb  100
Picos de Europa  146
Pio Cesare's Breakfast  72
Pissoirs  38
Plunkett Street  115
Poilane, Lionel  114
Pollock, Channing  149
Popcorn  38
Porn  38
Porridge  **84, 85**
Potato Bread  64
Poulard, La Mere  **70, 71**
Power, John David  54
Powersfield House  83
Pralines  38
Public Relations Consultants  158

**Quay House  33**
Quigley, Herb and Christine  **62, 75**

**Radishes  88**
Reggie Nadelson  53
Renvyle  40
Restaurant with Rooms  **31, 128**
Retro-Innovation  113
Rhubarb  **75, 82**
Ristorante Madonnina del Pescatore  73
Rival Hotel, Stockholm  38
Rocha John  **33, 135**
Roscarbery  54
Rosenthal  91
Ross Hotel, The  119
Rosslare  46
Roundwood House  100
Rue Cherche Midi  114

**Sandy Beach  144**
Schrager, Ian  136
Sexton, Regina  60
Shanagarry  74
Sheen Falls Lodge  125
Shelburne Lodge  137
Shorescape Seafoods  74
*Simple French Food*  69
Sligo, County  100

# INDEX

Slow Food  74

Smoked Haddock  76

Smoked Salmon  74

Sneem Black Pudding  54

Soda Bread  59

Soda Farls  66

Somers, Carmel  61

Spain  146

St. John's Point  30

Starck, Phillippe  136

Stockholm  **38, 136**

Strawberry Tree, The  113

Swallows, The  155

Sydney  **71, 146**

*Sydney Food*  **72, 84**

*Sydney Morning Herald*  71

**Tannery Restaurant, The**  73

Temple House  100

Temple Spa  40

Timoleague  74

Tipperary, County  **55, 75, 80, 89**

*Today Programme, The*  90

Tomatoes à la Polonaise  89

Traas, Con  80

Tramore  **33, 135**

Treacy, Janet  **112, 119**

Treacy, Padraig  **112, 119, 121**

*Tristan und Isolde*  91

Tuscany  164

**Ulster Fry**  57

Ummera Smokehouse  74

Uniquely Special Person  21

**Viel, Robert**  70

Visser, Margaret  34

von Bingen, Hildegard  91

**Walford, Rosie**  146

Wall Family, The  79

Walton's Mill  86

Wells Spa  118

West Cork  **33, 39, 40, 54, 61, 65, 74**

West Cork Hotel  76

West Waterford  **59, 77, 79**

West Waterford Good Food Tree  162

Wholemeal Bread  66

Wicklow, County  **92, 112**

*Wine Spectator*  155

WOM!  42

Woodcock Smokehouse  74

Word Of Mouth  42

Work-Life Balance  148

Wow! Factor  42

**Zurich**  84

# INDEX

# Recipes

American/Irish Breads  172
Angels on Horseback  176
Bannocks  66
Basted Eggs  181
Boxty  64
Bread  61-67, 170 172-175, 178
Breakfast Pancakes  68
Cinnamon Potato Buns  175
Clarified Butter  170
Crème Fraiche  170
Dilisk Bread  170
Eggs Benedict  171
Eggs en Cocotte  72
Eggs Ipanema, with Avocado and Fried Banana  176

Fadge  67
Finnan Haddie  78
French Toast  174
Fruit Compote, Winter  81
Granola  85
Hollandaise  180
Johnny Cakes with White pudding, Quail's Eggs and Spinach  177

Kedgeree  76

Lamb Kidneys in Grainy Mustard Sauce  79

Orange Hot Salad with Cinnamon and Honey  179
Oysters  89, 181
Oysters on Toast  89

Pancakes  68, 178
Potato Bread  64
Rhubarb & Grenadine Compote  82
Rhubarb Compote (to serve with smoked salmon)  75

Rye Bread, Spiced  172

Semolina Bread  173
Smoked Chicken Hash, Basted Eggs, Hollandaise, Sliced Melon  180
Smoked Haddock with Poached Eggs  78

Soda Bread, Chocolate and Cherry  63
Soda Bread, Flavoured  62
Soda Bread, Saffron and Sultana  63
Soda Bread, Wholemeal  61
Sourdough Pancakes, Quick  178
Toasted Muesli  85
Tomatoes à la Crème  88

# ALSO BY JOHN McKENNA

## THE HOW TO SERIES:

**HOW TO RUN A RESTAURANT**

– the companion volume to How to Succeed in Hospitality

The second edition of this critically acclaimed book analyses and explores the factors that must be understood in order to create a successful restaurant.

## THE BRIDGESTONE GUIDES SERIES:

The Bridgestone Irish Food Guide

The Bridgestone 100 Best Restaurants in Ireland

The Bridgestone 100 Best Places to Stay in Ireland

The Bridgestone Vegetarians' Guide to Ireland

The Bridgestone Food Lovers' Guide to Northern Ireland

Published by Estragon Press

# www.bridgestoneguides.com